Wondrous Love

Jamie,

May these words encourage you on your walk and lead you as you find hope in all things.

With Love,
Cynata
Compton

Wondrous Love

Author: Cynthia Complese

Foreword: by Lori Wolabaugh

Cover Art by: Deborah Nell

Published by Cynthia Complese
2017

All Scripture quotations, unless otherwise indicated, are taken from the New King James Bible ®. Copyright © 1982 by Thomas Nelson. Used by permission. All rights reserved.

Some italics in Scripture quotations reflect the author's added emphasis.

Details in some anecdotes and stories have been changed to protect the identities of the persons involved.

Copyright © 2017 by Cynthia Complese

All rights reserved. This book or any portion thereof may not be reproduced or used in any manner whatsoever without the express written permission of the publisher except for the use of brief quotations in a book review or scholarly journal.

First Printing: 2017

ISBN 978-1-5323-3514-3

Cynthia Complese
185 Newberry Commons #324
Etters, Pennsylvania 17319
www.PAMinistry.com

To every person with a silent cry, a quiet member
of a club no one wants to join, this book is for you.
May this help you find peace.

To every person who cannot imagine
being a part of the unthinkable, may this give
you a glimpse into how to help those you encounter.

Contents

Foreword xi
The Passing Shift 1
Moving Forward 29
Faith Propels Us 61
Learning to Heal 73
Walking It Out 81
Living Love Loud 89
Creative Value 97
About the Author 107
References 109

To my husband, for every encouraging
moment, word and smile.
You are my favorite, forever.

Foreword

Here in-lies the story of one woman's journey of love, joy, pain, loss, and hope. As you read these pages you will smile, cry, wonder, actually find it hard to put down as you come to know a mother's love and understand the love of our Jesus.

Jesus, who is always with us, walking each step of this pathway called life. He truly is that friend who stays by our side. We all go through seasons of our life we don't understand, and half the battle is knowing who you are and that you are not alone. But what happens when..... and yes, Cynthia asks these questions too. At any moment in our life a random situation can change our entire path giving us a new direction that we may not have been ready for. But he is there in that moment....waiting.

With the turn of each page you will experience her raw openness and feelings, that at times will take your breath away. You may ask yourself how can this be, is this for real? As I read on, tears would come but also a sense of renewed destiny. You will come to admire her strength, understand her passion for the arts and ability for life. Life is beautiful, it's fragile. Make memories, take time, you still have today.

This is Cynthia's story. No, not a story, it's more than that, it's a journey to where she found her place in God and the peace that has become her guide. I'm honored to have been asked by her to read her book and write the Forward. Here, in these pages, she shares her heart of a Wondrous Love.

Pastor Lori Wolabaugh
    February, 2017

Wondrous Love

1
The Passing Shift

February 21, 2011

Jeremy had left for bowling, and Josh had just laid down to sleep. I could hear him on the baby monitor and he rolled around, but not a sound was uttered. I knew I could have me time. I laid in bed and put on some random show on the TV. I had planned to veg the night away, but I couldn't. Something was still eating at me. I picked up the remote and turned the TV off and just sat there. No clue what it was that was on my mind, but something was stirring.

I laid back down, and began to have my first "conversation" with God.

"God, if you are real, I want to know" I paused and waited for an answer.

"I mean it, God, if you are real I am in, 100%, but if you aren't, I'm done!" I paused again.

Tears began to slowly roll down my cheeks as nothing was uttered back to me. Up until this point I could have told you there was an "Almighty Being", but I could not have told you His name. The Bible was just a story told to children so they would behave and angels and demons weren't real. But this night, I cried out to God. I had to know the truth.

I felt the tears fall faster and suddenly I was sobbing. I felt like I was going through the worst breakup of my life. Like the one I had loved forever and thought I would never be without was leaving me. I felt my heart break, as there was no response from God. I cried so hard I had to flip my pillow.

As I rolled on my side and sobbed, I felt it. A warm breath on my ear and God spoke my name "Cynthia". The tears that followed can only be described as a joyful weeping. God heard my cry, and came to me. I cried harder then I was before, and I was pretty certain I had run out of water in my body. I had stolen my husband's pillow because mine was officially drenched. That was the night, my heart turned back to God. That was the night that I knew, God was real.

"And you will seek Me and find Me, when you search for Me with all your heart." - Jeremiah 29:13

February 22, 2011

"Hi, this is Cynthia Complese, Joshua's mom. I just got a call from you guys."

"Hi Mrs. Complese, this is one of the teachers in Josh's room. He has a fever of 102 and needs to be picked up."

"Ok," I sighed, "I will have to make arrangements on that. I am
already in class at school, so it may be a few hours if his Grammy is unable to come get him. I can call you right back and let you know if you would like."

"That would be wonderful. Usually we set a firm 1 hour pick up rule, but the soonest you can get here the better. We understand."

"Thank you, I'll call you right back"

"Ok."

I got off the phone with them and called my mother in law right away.

"Hey, I just got a call from the daycare."

"Me too" she said, "I am on my way over to pick him up now."

"Ok, cool. I am already in class so as soon as class is over I will come get him from your place, if that's ok." I said

"That's fine, I will need to work later to make up for the time I am missing this morning though."

"Ok, I will try to not be late".

We said goodbye and I went back to class. Drawing 1 went by smoothly. Discussions of oil bars and ink wash filled my ears as I continued to work on my paper. I wasn't the greatest artist, but you could get the idea of what I was trying to portray. A few jokes with my classmates and some quick notes about homework and we were wrapping up class. My makeshift art box, that used to be a tackle box, closed tightly, and overflowing with supplies.

Arms full of art supplies and donut holes, I made my way to the car to pick up my little man from his Grammy's. The snow was still thick on the ground, but at least the walks were plowed and salted. Because the snow delayed my classes by 2 hours that morning, I decided to pick up donuts and coffee for my classmates. I loaded my supplies into the trunk and climbed in my car. I called Josh's pediatrician right away to schedule him for a doctor's appointment that afternoon. I didn't like that he was sick so suddenly.

The drive from the school to my mother in laws was slow, and my mind was filled with my class assignment and how we were going to work all this out now, because I was missing my required fitness class.

I pulled into the freshly plowed drive way at her house, parked in back and headed in the house, fiddling with the back door so I wouldn't drop the donuts. I figured she would be able to take them to work and the guys there would eat them. I got in the house and Josh smiled at me that wonderful, heart melting smile. How could I not smile back to him? I was waiting for the request for food. I knew it was coming.

"Mooorrre?" he said, pointing at the donut box.

"You want a donut?" I asked him, returning that amazing smile he gave me.

"Donu!" he replied, very happily. You would not have known he was sick.

So I handed him a small glazed donut hole from the box, as his Grammy and I tried to figure out our schedules so that I can go to my 5:30 class tonight. He had one in each hand by the time he walked away and a big smile on his little face, off to play with every single toy he had in his toy box there.

"Doos!" he said, leaving his little car garage in the living room with toy cars scattered all around it.

Cynthia Complese

"Ok, we'll get you some juice buddy. You want apple juice?" I asked him, knowing full well that was his favorite.

"Appl doos" he told us as his Grammy was already filling a sippy cup. His donuts were gone and he drank down a good bit of juice. "mooorrr" he told us as he reached for the donuts, his appetite had not changed in the least.

"Ok, my sweet, let's get you one for each hand" Grammy told him as she grabbed two more donut holes for him. We were both smiling at him as he took them from her and escaped to his toy car garage again.

"Tank-oo, Griea" he said as he walked away.

"Get some rest, buddy" I said as I kissed his little forehead and tucked him into his fire engine bed. He smiled at me and snuggled into his favorite blanket, hand crocheted by his great-grandma. I closed the door to his room and headed off down stairs to my car to get my lunch. We had just come home from the doctor's and Josh was exhausted. I figured we would grab a quick drive thru lunch and come home. Josh fell asleep in the back seat on the way home, which was not normal for him. So I had left my lunch in the car and decided to carry him upstairs and tuck him in. Ultimately deciding to eat a cold meal, that used to be hot. Which was normal for me, Josh came first and I would eat when he was done or we would share a meal.

I took my fast food bag and headed upstairs toward the computer room. Passing his room as I went down the hall, I could hear him sound asleep and lightly snoring. I settled into my computer chair and started up my computer. My husband and I enjoy playing online games when we are not playing the role of Mommy and Daddy, so spending free time at the computer was not unheard of in our house. I ate my cold fries and sandwich and drank my watered-down soda. It wasn't too bad. I kept thinking about why Josh did not want to eat his lunch, he just handed it back to me. That was not normal for him. He loved to eat and had a healthy appetite.

His doctor told us today that he had a viral infection and pink eye. So, we had filled his script for eye drops and picked up lunch. I didn't think it was bad enough for him to turn down fries, but it seems it was. Things just didn't seem to add up, but Josh had never really been sick before, so I wasn't sure what to expect.

Wondrous Love

    I checked my email and responded to some of them, then checked my Facebook briefly. I felt a sudden urge to go check in on Josh, but the urge was quickly shrugged off. I knew I was on limited time so I figured I would get on the video game and say hi to some friends before getting into my homework. Jeremy and I were talking back and forth online. We always seem to have the best conversations through email, messaging, and text. A few minutes out of the game and I felt the nudge in my heart to check on Josh again. I dismissed it once more, saying to myself "he's fine". I began looking over some homework that was due the next day. Running final details through my head and making notes. I felt the nudge again, a little stronger.

> "Then He said, "Go out, and stand on the mountain before the Lord." And behold, the Lord passed by, and a great and strong wind tore into the mountains and broke the rocks in pieces before the Lord, but the Lord was not in the wind; and after the wind an earthquake, but the Lord was not in the earthquake; and after the earthquake a fire, but the Lord was not in the fire; and after the fire *a still small voice.*"
> - 1 Kings 19:11-12

    I had decided I needed to get off the computer anyway. It was about 4pm and I knew I had a 5:30pm class and I did not want to be late dropping Josh off with his Grammy. It never took much effort to get him out the door once he knew where he was going. Josh loves Jeremy's parents very much.
    I went to his room where the little blue lamp was on, like usual, because he didn't like sleeping in the dark. The little space heater on his dresser had just turned off as I walked up to the side of his bed. I rubbed his back gently and softly whispered his name, bending over so he could hear me. He was lying a little weird, I noticed, as I spoke to him a little louder.
    "Josh, buddy. It's time to get up" I said rubbing his back a bit stronger. I turned away to switch off the lamp and heater, thinking he would sit up like he usually does. Because I had felt a twitch in his back like he had moved I didn't think twice about it, until I turned around. He was still laying in his bed on his stomach. I ran over to him and rolled him over. His body was limp and his lips were turning purple, panic hit my mind as I screamed his name.

    "JOSHUA!" his name rang from my lips like a horror movie scream. I scooped him up in my arms, feeling his arms lay limp at his side as I held his head still with my left hand. I ran down

Cynthia Complese

the stairs to the living room, where my cell phone had been charging. His body was lifeless and limp as I laid him on the floor by his small couch, my hands shook slightly as my fingers dialed the numbers, 9-1-1.

"911, what is your emergency?"

"My son, he isn't responding and he's limp and his lips are turning purple!" I frantically told the lady who took the call, my heart was racing at this point.

"Ok, where are you at?" She calmly told me

"At home, in New Cumberland" I continued to tell her my home address.

"Ok, we have someone on the way, how old is your son?"

"He's two!" I told her.

"I want you to put your ear near his mouth and nose and tell me if you hear him breathing."

"Ok" I set the phone away from my ear so I could focus on listening for his breath. My ear brushing against his nose slightly, nothing. "He's not breathing, and I don't know CPR!"

"Ok, I want you to lay him flat on his back and lift his chin up slightly. Do you see anything in his mouth or throat?" she asked me calmly.

I lifted his chin and opened his mouth. "No I don't see anything", my voice was still frantic.

"Ok, next I want you to pinch his nose closed and blow air into his mouth to fill his lungs, you are going to do this twice." She continued to methodically explain every step to me.

"Ok" I pinched his little nose with my thumb and first finger and pressed my mouth against his, as I blew warm air into his mouth. I heard it enter his mouth like wind going down a tunnel, and saw from the corner of my eye as his chest lifted slightly. I stopped, lifted my head for a moment, took another breath in and did it, filling his lungs with air for him once more.

Wondrous Love

"Ok, I did it" I told the 911 dispatcher.

"Alright, next I am going to have you take the heel of your right hand and place it over his chest, just below where the rib cage meets. You're going to push 30 times, I want you to put me on speaker and count out loud to me."

"Ok" I pushed the speaker button on my phone and laid it on the opposite side of Josh from me. I pushed on his chest, "1... 2.... 3.... 4.... 5... " I spoke aloud. Time seemed to slow during this, but all I could think of was saving my baby boy. "... 18... 19.... 20.... 21..." My poor baby boy, lying here, lifeless. "28.... 29.... 30".

"Ok, now I want you to lift his chin and check for anything in his mouth or throat."

I lifted his chin again and looked in his mouth, "No, I don't see anything" my panic had turned to concern.

"I want you to pinch his nose and give two strong breaths into his mouth again"

"Ok" I pinched his nose and gave a good breath into his mouth. I heard it fill his lungs. I gave a second breath, and I heard it fill his lungs and then I was startled away....

BAM! BAM! I thought my front door was about to come off it's hinges. In one fluid motion, I pulled away from Joshua's side and grabbed my phone as I ran to the door. My front door swung open as I reached it and I had to stop abruptly to not be hit by it.

"Did you call an Ambulance?" A man at my door said to me, ready to rush in my home, with several others behind him standing on my steps.

"YES! In here!" I responded frantically, moving from the door so they could get in.

"They are here, the ambulance is here! Thank You!" I told the 911 dispatcher as I hung up the phone to attend to the ambulance and give them as much info that I could.

An officer pulled me aside, so that the EMT's could do their job in reviving my son. We stepped over to a doorway, just a few feet away, that led into another room.

"What happened?" the officer asked me, as calm as possible.

"I..." I started to shake and my breathing became difficult. I still had not cried or thought about the situation yet. I kept looking past the officer to what was going on with Josh, just 4 feet from me.

"Calm down, take your time" The office reassured me, with a calm, steady voice.

"I went in to wake my son from his nap and when I shook him he wouldn't wake up. I rolled him over and his lips were purple and he wasn't breathing. So, I scooped him up and brought him down here and called 911..." I continued to recount the moments up until they arrived.

Suddenly the EMT's scooped up my son in their arms and ran out the door with him. Opposite the man that carried was another that was using a bulbous item to rush air into his lungs.

"What hospital are they going to?" I asked the officer, who in turn asked the EMT's.

"Do you have a preference?" the EMT's asked me.

"Harrisburg Hospital"

"Ok" they responded and they were out the door.

"Can I go with him?" I asked the officer. I felt panicked as I quickly tried to figure out what to do if they said no, I could not imagine leaving him.

The officer turned and asked someone from the ambulance "Can mom ride along?"

"Yes" Said a gentleman I had not seen before.
I started to follow him to the ambulance when the officer stopped me, "You need shoes."

Wondrous Love

I bolted from the living room to the dining room and put on the easiest shoes I owned, slip on tennis shoes. I grabbed my book bag that I knew had my wallet in it and ran back to the front door, my cell phone was still in my hand.

"Do you have keys to get back in"

"Yes" I told the officer, while I wasn't sure if I did or not, I knew my husband did.

"Ok, we'll lock up for you" the officer told me, as I walked out the front door, down the porch and climbed into the ambulance.

I got in the front seat of the ambulance and time slowed. I tried to call my husband 3 times, but I could not get through. So I called my mother in law.

"I need you to call Jeremy and tell him to get to Harrisburg Hospital. Josh isn't breathing"

"What happened?" she asked, I could hear the panic in her voice.

"I don't know, we are in the ambulance on the way over now."

"Ok" she said as we hung up.

Moments passed and I tried my husband's work again... nothing. I tried his cell phone one more time. Ring one... "he hasn't left yet" I started to think. Ring two... "he isn't going to pick up." Ring three... "voice mail is coming again".

"Hello?"

"Jeremy!" I couldn't explain the feeling of relief that came over me when he picked up, but I felt like I wasn't alone anymore. "Did your mom get a hold of you?"

"Yes, she did, what happened?" concern was brimming in his voice.

"I don't know, Josh was unresponsive from nap and I called 911. We're in the ambulance outside the house right now. Where are you at?"

Cynthia Complese

"I'm at the top of the mountain now, should be passing the house soon", he was amazingly calm, and I could hear he was still driving.

"Ok, well just go straight to the hospital."
"Ok"

"I love you", I wanted to start to cry.

"I love you" He responded softly, as we hung up. I don't know what went through his mind, but I had to let him know I love him.

I kept looking at the driver asking what was happening. The ambulance had not moved from the spot in front of my house and I knew we needed to get to a hospital. The sirens had not started yet, but I could see the lights flashing by reflection from the window on my screen door. After what felt like 50 minutes, but they said was only 5 minutes, the ambulance started to move and the sirens blared into action. I buckled up as we went down the main road toward the interstate. It wasn't long before I was racing along the side of the stretcher that my little boy was laying on, as someone was pumping his chest with their hand and another was squeezing a bag that was connected to a hose in his mouth. We raced through the hospital until we were back in the ER. They wheeled him into a room and I froze just outside of the doorway. I watched as nurses and doctors rushed into his room past me.

A nurse came to me and asked "Are you mom?", very caringly.

"Yes, I am." I responded to her with a shaky voice, as I peered past her to the team that was rapidly working on my little Joshua.

"What's his name?" she asked as she turned back to look in the room.

"Joshua" I said as tears started to swell in my eyes. I was finally starting to cry. My left hand shook as I wiped a tear from my cheek.

"Ok, does Joshua have a history of allergies or cardiac troubles?" she had a clipboard in her arm and her hand was

Wondrous Love

ready to take notes. It was almost like she was expecting me to list off a roll call of issues.

"No, he's healthy" I told them as the doctor came up behind the woman. She told the doctor what I just said. He turned to me with a caring look in his eyes.

"We'll take good care of him, ok?"

I nodded. Tears flooded my face, stopping any words from coming from my mouth. The words I needed to hear at this point, was just that. That he was going to be in good hands.

"Do you want to stay near Joshua or in the waiting room?" The nurse asked me.

"I'd like to stay nearby if I can"

"Most certainly! Let's just find you a chair" Another nurse went with her in search of chairs. They found two and brought them next to the doorway of the room where Joshua was.

"His... His dad is on the way, he should be here any minute." I told them.

"Ok, we'll let them know out at the front desk, what's his first name?"

"Jeremy."

"Ok, we'll be sure to bring him back."

I sat down on the chair that was next to his doorway and just spaced out and breathed. At this point I am sure my eyes had a glazed over look to them. I didn't know what to do or what to think. I could feel my hands shaking and I am sure my face looked a little pale.

"Can I get you anything?" a nurse asked me.

"Umm... some... some water would be nice." I couldn't think, I
almost didn't process what she had said.

"Water? You got it!" and she hurried away.

Cynthia Complese

I just sat there, a blank stare. I didn't even have a place to start for my mind to race. Not even a "what if" filled my mind. For the first time, I could ever remember, I didn't think of anything. I was officially in shock. She came back with my water at the same time a doctor came to talk to me.

"Can you tell me what happened?" The doctor asked.

I stepped him through everything. From the time, I got a call about a fever, to carrying him upstairs, to the second we walked in the hospital. Every detail I could recall I said as calmly as I could, tears coming slowly.

"Ok, we're going to get him stable and they are going to do a chest x-ray and then I'll be back to talk to you, ok?"

I nodded. I didn't know what was going on or why this happened. My brain was trying to put things together and try to think things through, but I couldn't comprehend what my brain was trying to put together.

Jeremy came through a set of electric double doors, escorted by a nurse. As he came over to me, another nurse and a doctor were coming to speak with me. They informed us that Josh was breathing with assistance from a machine and that they were going to have him transferred to the Penn State Children's Hospital.

"Would you like to see him?" they asked us, gingerly. A level of uncertainty in the doctor's voice.

"Yes" I said, with a nod, as tears began to swell once more.

I stepped through the room and saw him lying there, lifeless. His clothes had been cut off him and he was in just a diaper. I took his hand in mine and began to weep. My husband was at my side with his right hand on my back for comfort and his left hand on Josh.

"You can talk to him" a nurse said to us, as she checked on his IV.

"Hey, Buddy." I said to him through a shaking voice. "Mama's here... and Daddy's here too." Tears came freely at this point and I almost couldn't breathe. Meanwhile a nurse came in and was speaking with the doctor.

Wondrous Love

"Do you know how much he weighs?" the nurse asked the doctor.

"39 pounds even." I piped in "he was weighed today at the doctor's appointment." My swollen eyes still pushing out tears, looked over at the doctor. I could feel the burning, from crying too hard.

The doctor nodded at me and then to the nurse.

I stood there for a few more moments and then the X-ray team arrived. I stepped out into the hallway with Jeremy and we waited. We knew that Josh was going to be moved to a different hospital. Jeremy took this moment to go let his parents know the status, I waited there for him to come back.

I was told it was only a few hours later, but it seemed like it took much longer, the transport team arrived. I was told it was a special team from Hershey. The driver was wonderful with me and very understanding. Jeremy drove our car over to Hershey and his parents drove in their car while I rode with Joshua in the ambulance. I couldn't handle the idea of not being near him.

I had to clear my mind from his fragile body in the back and how delicate he seemed now. I started to think of when we he was first born. How the doctors were all concerned about him being 4 weeks early and that he might not have been able to breath, but that he came out wailing. Now here we were, and he wasn't breathing. I had to get my mind on something else. I started asking questions to the driver, anything I could think of. She told me she was just a regular ambulance driver, but the people in back were part of a life line team. They rode in helicopters and if they had decided to move Josh by helicopter, I would not have been able to ride with him. I didn't know that. Soon we were arriving at Hershey and I was dropped off in a waiting room as the sped off into a locked area, the PICU. I saw Jeremy and his parents coming down the hallway as we got off the elevator that was directly in front of the family room.

They told me to wait in the family room and someone would be back soon. So I sat down, and waited... and waited... and waited. Nurses and Doctors came back and asked question after question. I told them the same thing over and over and over about what happened. Nothing changed. Sometimes I would remember a small detail, but nothing ever changed. I just kept having to relive finding my son unresponsive in his bed. Every

Cynthia Complese

time they asked me what happened I would start to crumble and fall apart... sometimes I couldn't even breath. They would wait patiently for me to recompose myself, or Jeremy would pipe in. He had heard everything enough times to know what happened.

Josh was brought into Hershey Hospital at 9pm, after many issues with getting an IV and line in him and getting his vent hose changed out and everything, I was finally able to go see him. It was 2am at this point. Jeremy and I went back and loved on him some, our minds were exhausted. The doctors expressed their concerns about not knowing how long he had been without oxygen. Jeremy and I were still in shock at what was going on.

The morning of the incident, Joshua was the happiest little boy in the world. He ran up to his daddy and gave him a big hug and said "Bye Dadda" and then he and I left out the back door, and now he was lying lifeless on this bed. We just took in the situation and walked out of the PICU in Hershey Med Children's Hospital.

Jeremy and I talked about the night and what are plan was at this point. I decided I was not leaving the hospital and Jeremy was going to head home to try to get some sleep before work the next day. He was going to try to make it in. I tried to curl up on a hard couch that night in the family room. It was uncomfortable and restless and I was up very early. I headed straight back to be with my baby boy.

I was there in time to see the new Doctor doing his rounds. They stopped and spoke with me and let me know they were sending Josh back for a head CT that morning to see the status of his brain. Our new doctor was amazing. They had swapped shifts that morning and we had a new doctor for the week.

After talking with Josh and kissing his hands and forehead for a bit, I went out into the family room and called Jeremy.

"They are going to be sending Josh back for head CT this morning. They said he will go back around ten."

"Oh," Jeremy started, "I wasn't expecting them to start testing already."

"I know, I thought they would wait a few days or something."

"I'll jump in the shower and head out." Jeremy informed me.

"Sounds good. I need to call my parents; can you call yours and let them know?"

"Yup."

Wondrous Love

"Ok, thanks. I love you."

"I love you."

"mm..bye" I said, as was our standard notice of 'I'm hanging up'.

"mm..bye" he replied.

I plugged my cell phone in and began dialing the number to my
parents. As I listened to their phone ring I didn't know how to let them know what was going on. I had called them the night before while we were waiting to let them know Josh was in the hospital and where we were. Now I had to let them know that Josh was going back for a head CT. My dad answered and I told him, somehow it came out. He said they were flying out that day and should be here by that night. My heart lifted, I was happy my parents were coming out to be with me.

I sat down on a couch and began sending out the texts. I had so many to send. I started with one mass text, but not everyone's numbers fit in it, so I had to send out two. The list seemed never ending and keeping everyone up to date was difficult, time consuming and stressing. I just kept hoping I didn't forget anyone important.

Time began to lapse, I faded in and out of a half sleep state and soon Jeremy and his parents were with me and we were sitting in the family room. Jeremy's best friends (they might as well be brothers) texted to say there were on their way out as well. They asked if we needed anything and I said I was fine. They offered to bring us lunch and I told them whatever sounded fine.

Jeremy's mom ran to the pharmacy for us to get some basics for me and him. Like shampoo, deodorant, mine and Jeremy's medications and I asked if she would get a birthday card for my mom. When all this happened, I had not gotten the chance to call my mom and tell her Happy Birthday. Josh went into the Hospital on my mom's birthday. I knew it was mute at this point, I knew her birthday would be unforgettable now, but I had to try to bring a smile to her face still.

I sat in the waiting room watching as Josh was wheeled past. They had a full support system for him, including back up medications, batteries and extra nurses. Joshua was on full life support and detailed as being in a coma. They had given him a sedative on day one, but they stopped it. They said they were waiting for him to over breath the ventilator before having to se-

Cynthia Complese

date him. He wasn't over breathing or even trying to. I remember stopping them as they wheeled past, just briefly, to give him a kiss on his little forehead. I remember it was still cool from the hypothermia protocol they had started him on.

Hypothermia protocol is used after cardiac arrest, when the patient has gone without oxygen and is at risk of brain damage. Using cooling pads and gel pads they cool the body from 37 degrees Celsius to 32 – 34 degrees Celsius within the first 2 -3 hours and is maintained for 24 – 48 hours after the arrest. At which point the body is slowly rewarmed at 1 degree every 4 – 6 hours back up to the normal temperature.

    I came back in the family room and sat down. Jeremy's best friends Ben and Chris arrived shortly after Josh went for his head CT. I was so thankful for their arrival and still am. I had not eaten since lunch the day before and they reminded me how important it was for me to take care of myself. They had brought fast food with them for lunch and I remember eating a sandwich and just calming my mind.
    We talked for some time in the family room. It was good to see Jeremy laughing and talking, he had been so quiet and his friends always bring a smile to his face. I remember the guys were in the middle of laughing about something when we saw them bring Joshua past. I stood up and walked with them for a second and asked how soon I could come back to be with him again. They told me to give them about 30 minutes to get him situated again and then it should be fine. So back in the family room I went, letting the family and friends there know what was going on.
    Thirty minutes lasted forever, but soon we could go back to see him again. When we went back, Josh's nurse informed us that it would be a few hours before we got the results of the head CT. We were fine with that and continued on with loving and praying over Josh. Jeremy and I went back to the family room so Jeremy's mom could go back and be with Joshua for a bit. Her and I decided we were not allowed to be back there together, because we turned into one big waterfall at his side. Our love for Josh is amazing in and of itself, together we were a mess, plus the PICU had a rule of no more than 2 people back at a time.
    Time passed as we laughed and talked, being with friends eased the pain some. Soon the doctor had let us know they had received the results of Josh's head CT and would like to speak with Jeremy and I alone in a moment. My heart raced and I

Wondrous Love

grabbed Jeremy's hand and just held onto it. I didn't know what to expect.

A few minutes took forever and soon Jeremy and I were walking back into the PICU to see what the Doctor had for us, hand in hand. I couldn't let go, even when we sat down with the doctor behind a computer desk and he started to pull up Josh's CT results. I think I may have even held on tighter.

He began to explain the results and I felt my heart sink and tears swell. They showed us that his CT revealed that his brain was swollen, very swollen. Where there should have been ripples and waves on his brain, it was so swollen it was showing as flat. My tears began to roll down my cheeks as I felt Jeremy squeeze my hand. A nurse came by and handed me tissue and I just kept crying.

"On the CT where there should be fluid it appears black, but as you can see on this image it appears slightly grayed and is actually much smaller than it should be. Which is where we have concern about whether that is infection and his brain being so swollen that it is pushing the fluid out."

Josh's doctor explained these results and I remember crying as the truth sunk in. He told us there was a slim chance that the swelling could come down, but that he would not be the same afterward.

"Ummm... what... what are our best chances?" I barely could get out of my mouth.

"Best case results would be him living, but being severely brain damaged and not capable of self-surviving."

Tears rolled heavily now and I was shaking. I was sobbing so hard I was starting to feel sick to my stomach. Jeremy and I were soon walking out of the PICU, still hand in hand. We had to let everyone know these results, everyone that was waiting in the family room and this was the hardest part, the texts didn't involve seeing people or them seeing me.

We stopped just outside the PICU and spoke briefly. Comforting each other and trying to compose ourselves as best we could. Jeremy and I, while married and loving each other, were not that close. Not as close as others might have expected.

We walked into the family room, where his mom and dad were and Chris and Ben. Thankfully it was just them, but that was difficult enough. I stood in front of a counter, that had a mirror and closets on either side. Jeremy headed over and sat down next to his friends and started, I piped in where I needed to. We all knew what we weren't saying, that the outcome was grim and sad.

"Best case, he would be dependent on us forever, unable to feed himself, dress himself..." Jeremy stated as tears came on hard for him. Chris put his arm around him to comfort him. He started to cry and I followed in suit. Emotions were high and tears came warm and freely.

"I don't care, we'll take him however he is, no matter what" one of his parents had said, you could hear their heart breaking.

Jeremy and I had both decided that Josh deserved so much more than being an "ornament in the corner" and deserved a life. This was part of the discussion we had before telling everyone the results. I prayed in my heart, that if that was to be his outcome, then for God to take him where he could laugh and play in heaven and not be chained on earth.

"For this is the will of God, that by doing good you may put to silence the ignorance of foolish men" - 1 Peter 2:15

I texted this to my sister and let her know that I didn't want it sent out to the family yet. Our parents were flying in from Lakewood, WA that night and I didn't want it to get back to them yet. I didn't want the family to think I was keeping them out of the loop for no reason, I just didn't want my mom and dad to worry about it while they were in flight. I also wanted to wait for them to arrive for me to tell them what was going on face to face and have the chance to answer questions.

The rest of the day slowed. They said they would be doing an EEG that night and we would have results within 24 hours. So, we began to wait for the next test results. Jeremy's friends left, then his parents left and it was just us the rest of the night. Courtney, my spiritual backbone and dearest friend, surprised us that night by coming by to pray over Josh. I didn't have a strong belief system and I didn't know who I was in Christ, in fact I had not read a bible since my preteen years. But here she was, coming into a hospital to pray for Josh. Her son was my son's best friend and had been through a lot in his few years. Several heart surgeries and illnesses had lead her on an amazing spiritual journey, and she was here in spite of concerns, to pray for my son. My heart swelled with love and joy at the sight of her. I almost ran to greet her. Jeremy sat in the waiting room as I walked back with her. She was familiar with the PICU and the nursing staff there, in fact many of them knew her by name. We put on

Wondrous Love

the yellow gowns, that they request we wear and headed to the last bed on the right. That was Josh's bed. The nurse was updating his chart with information and Courtney stood at the foot of his bed while I held his hand and talked to him. I spent a few moments in silence, my heart praying what I did not have words for, then we walked back out. My gratitude for Courtney being there and supporting in this way, was beyond words.

Soon after Courtney left, Jeremy was leaving for our home to get some sleep. He was not comfortable sleeping in public. I kissed him goodnight and I curled up on a couch, as I waited to hear from my parents that they landed. It was around 1:30 the morning of the 24th when I got the text message that they had landed and checked into their hotel room. They were now on the way to Hershey Hospital. Immediately following their text I received a text from the Bishop of the Mormon church, he too was on his way.

I made my way to the main entrance of the hospital and waited for them to arrive. The receptionist was gone and the counter they sat behind was empty. The wheelchairs were cluttered in their corner and the automated door was only available to let people out, coming in was locked. The Bishop arrived first, and we spoke a little as I got a wheel chair ready for my mom, because the walk back to the Children's Hospital was long and her body did not have the strength for it. Soon my parents arrived and Dad dropped mom at the entrance, then parked the car. Mom and I made small talk with the Bishop from the church while waiting for Dad to come back. Mom was always good at socializing. Once we were all in the hospital and dad was pushing mom's wheelchair, I began to explain where we were at. I had made arrangements to be able to take them all back with me to see Josh at the same time, so to his bedside we went.

It was more visible to see the pain in mom than in dad, although mom tried to hide it and dad was always the best at hiding it. I knew they were both hurting, I knew because I was hurting. I spoke to Josh and introduced him to his Nana and Papa. Their first meeting was now, while he laid in this bed unable to show them the amazing personality we had all grown to know and love. My heart ached at this, that they had not met him while he was so active. The Bishop and my father prayed over Josh and then we headed back to the hallway, the one leading to the family room. They stayed for about an hour and we spoke. The bishop walked with my parents and I as we headed to the main entrance. I said my goodnights and went back up to the family room. I sat in the dining area of the two-family rooms at a computer and began to build a CarePage for Joshua.

Cynthia Complese

I was so stressed out with sending updates to everyone every 5 minutes and I knew I couldn't get notices out to everyone. One of my dearest friends told me about CarePages and I began to build a page for just Josh. I filled out his information and then at 4:35 am I made the following post.

"We want to thank everyone for their prayers and thoughts. We still have not been given results of the EEG they had done. The preliminary results do not look good, but we are uplifting Josh to God and through Christ we are praying that he will be healed and his brain will be healed.

My parents have arrived to meet Josh. They left only an hour ago. With news that Josh is down to 1 BP med from 4 and his sugars are down by half and his oxygen percent is down 35% (which is good) and his BP is up, our prayers go to the Lord in Christ's name that Joshua's brain will be healed. That at this point he is in God's hands and They will heal him. Josh has not shown signs of over breathing the ventilator since yesterday morning and has not been on the Versed since 9am yesterday. Which means he is not chemically induced in this coma and that his unresponsiveness is not from medication.

So we are praying, Dear Lord, that you will touch his head and kiss his face and heal his brain. That through your Son, Christ, he will be healed and he will be whole. That he will come back to us and show us he is fighting, that through Him we will find our hope and cling to it. That we will see a shimmer of light and grab shovels and at Christ's side we will dig Josh out, with Christ and Holy Spirit guiding our hearts.

"God, we know this is too big for us, but we know this is not too big for you! So we ask, in Christ's name, heal his Brain."

Love, Cynthia and Jeremy"

I finished my time at the computer by sending out a mass email to everyone and posting on Facebook. I wanted everyone to know about this page. This was how we were going to be sending out updates, and I didn't want anyone to be kept in the dark. I coveted prayers at this point, and I was not going to turn away anyone willing to pray for my son.

I laid myself down on a couch and tried to catch a few moments of sleep. It was 5 hours later when Jeremy returned and with him, breakfast. We ate some and talked some, my appetite was not there. Soon my parents arrived and so did Jeremy's. Tension came with their arrivals, because everyone was emotional and trying to be strong. I think both our parents felt like they had the duties of being strong, especially our mothers. My

Wondrous Love

parents passed time reading on their kindles, Jeremy's mom went back to be with Joshua and Jeremy and I took turns on the laptop and played on our phones. All we could do... is wait. Amidst the waiting, we received a text from Jeremy's friend, Chris. He was in the hospital, mama was in labor and his baby boy was on the way!

It was slow going as the time ticked by. By 11am I asked Jeremy if he would be willing to come down to the chapel with me. I had to clear my head and relax, I wasn't sleeping and I felt drained and weak. He said sure so we gathered up and walked down. It was a slow walk, but it was nice to just get up and move. It was also nice to be together. To feel the comfort of his voice and the feel of his hand in mine, or on my back. We got down to the chapel and I sat on the floor, I felt I needed to humble myself before God. My legs were crossed and I turned to sort of face Jeremy but to also kind of face the center, where they had a small fountain going. The sound of which was soothing.

I closed my eyes and started to clear my thoughts. As I did I saw something I didn't really understand. Clear as day, as though I was physically standing there, I saw Joshua, standing on his bed. There were no cords or wires attached and his arms were rested out at his sides. I saw him look at me and I felt like he was saying to me "Look Mama! Look what I can do!". My eyes popped open, I was still sitting in the chapel, Jeremy was on the chair in front of me playing on his phone. So, I closed my eyes again and it was gone. I couldn't bring it back, no matter how hard I tried, all I had now was the memory. At that moment, I opened my eyes and stood up. I didn't know what to think of this, so I told Jeremy. He wasn't sure either.

"At least he is still here." I remember telling him. Later sharing what I had seen with my friend Courtney.

"And it shall come to pass afterward
That I will pour out My Spirit on all flesh;
Your sons and your daughters shall prophesy,
Your old men shall dream dreams,
Your young men shall see visions.
And also on My menservants and on My maidservants
I will pour out My Spirit in those days." - Joel 2:28-29

We went back upstairs and went back to see Josh. He was laying there, still and quiet. Breathing tube in his mouth, IV in his arm... nothing had changed. But something had changed in me, I had more hope now than I did before. The doctor came over to us and pulled us aside for a moment to speak. Giving us the details of the day. Which we in turn posted on CarePages, here is the post from that moment.

"Posted Feb 24, 2011 2:39pm

Well, the blood cultures finally produced a result. It was confirmed that Joshua has H1N1 Flu. It's possible that it was H1N1 by itself, which moved to his brain. The other main possibility is that the H1N1 lowered his immune system enough for meningitis to kick in. We have no way to confirm or rule out meningitis right now.

Another item of note is that he was warmed up today to see if there would be any difference. After warming him up to 36°C, Joshua's pupil rippled when a light was shined in his eye. He also had a reaction when his shoulder was pinched. The doctor said that the reaction to the shoulder pinch was likely a "spinal reaction", rather than a brain reaction. There was no reaction when Josh's ear was pinched, which would have proven a brain reaction. The doctor also stated that neither of these reactions were reason for hope, but we're still being hopeful that more and better things will come.

Since there was some change when Josh was warmed, they are cooling him back down and continuing the hypothermia protocol. They're doing this for another 9-10 hours. Hopefully this will result in some of the brain swelling coming down and some more function returning. We'll wait and see; hope and pray.

Thank you all for your continued support. It really does mean very much to us.
-- Jeremy"

The day dragged on. My mom and I headed across the street from the Hospital to the Ronald McDonald house and set up a place for Jeremy and I to stay. Mom put it under their name, but left the room for just us, so that Jeremy and I could stay close to Josh and have a place to ourselves. Her and dad stayed at a hotel just a few blocks away. By the time, we returned we still had not heard from the from the Cardiologist about the echocardiogram. We spent most of the day up in the family room, with our parents. Just talking and waiting. In the middle of the bad something good came in, we got a call from Jeremy's best friend, Chris. His little boy Braden was born at 5:52pm. It was welcomed news as many of us wanted something to keep our mind off the gloom that seemed to surround us.

Posted Feb 24, 2011 7:43pm

"Well, we just sat down with the cardiologist about the echocardiogram. He said that when he examined the results, he noticed a long QT. I can only explain long QT the way he explained it to us. Each time the heart beats, it has a "reset" triggered, and then beats again. The long QT can affect the "reset" between heart beats. In most people, this can exist as Long QT Syndrome for years or decades without a problem. For other people, it can cause a fibrillation, which can cause many heart problems, including cardiac arrest.

The cardiologist isn't sure whether this is Long QT Syndrome, which would have existed prior to this incident, or whether it's just a long QT due to the brain injury. If it's due to the brain injury, it may be temporary or permanent. If it was from prior to the incident, it will be permanent.

The cardiologist examined all of today's heart monitor printouts and said that his heart rhythm looks fine. He said that this will not likely be a problem for Josh, but it's something that we should know about. He also suggested that we both get echocardiograms and have a genetic test from Josh's blood. If either of us are found to have Long QT Syndrome, it's helpful for two things: we know of a condition that we have and it's much more likely that Josh's is genetic/pre-existing. If neither of us have Long QT Syndrome, then we're back to where we are now. The genetic test would take a few weeks and would show if Josh has any genetic markers for Long QT Syndrome.

Essentially, this is just more information. The cardiologist said he believes that its most likely a result of the brain injury, rather than a pre-existing condition. He believes it's even less likely to be the cause of all of this. The cardiologist was really more concerned with us finding out if we have it.

Anyway, it was more information, so we figured we'd share. If you have questions, let us know!"

We spoke about the issues with our family and thankful that the results were otherwise good. We went back and kissed Josh goodnight and headed to get some rest at the Ronald McDonald House.

Knowing we needed this time to rest and very thankful to my parents for setting us up there. I don't know how I would have handled being there with no escape to breathe and spending every night apart.

Cynthia Complese

Posted Feb 24, 2011 10:53pm

"Tomorrow we end the 48 hour hypothermia protocol. We are taking tonight to rest up, as we know tomorrow will be a day of trials. Today was a day for strength and building our relationship with God and Christ. We know that we are in for trials tomorrow and that our faith may be pushed to the max. So we are going to sleep tonight and pray and face tomorrow with a fresh mind and spirit.

We thank all of you that are reading this page, spending time with us and praying with us. We have decided we are at a point we are not turning people away who want to come and be with us. The comfort is so great, that we are welcoming it.

I am asking one thing tonight, that as you take your moment to reach out to Christ and pray, that you take a half a second and ask in Christ's name, that we will see a positive turn. I cannot stop saying it, but through Christ Josh will be healed, and we will watch before our eyes as God will make Josh's body whole.

My faith is strengthened every day, as I pray and I feel angels guard our boy. I was told that heaven will open up when we pray in Christ's name. So tonight I am praying, "Lord bring us change, bring us positive change. In Christ's name we ask that you bind all that is stifling the good and remove it from his body. That you embrace us as we get news and you keep us strong. That you continue to heal his brain, in Christ's name. Holy Holy Holy God Almighty. Amen""

But the salvation of the righteous is from the Lord;
He is their strength in the time of trouble. - Psalm 37:39

We put the laptop away and went to sleep. Hoping for a refreshing morning. We woke early, the alarm was set so that we could meet my parents for breakfast before heading over. I got up and jumped in the shower while Jeremy slept a little longer. Then I got out and woke Jeremy so he could get in. It was nice to sleep in a real bed and get a real shower, one that was not shared with a public bathroom. Jeremy's mom was awesome and bought us some shampoo and things from Rite Aid the day before. I had finished getting dressed and was looking out the large window in our room when suddenly I saw Jeremy and I walking through the front door of the hospital. We had every color behind us, like when you put your face too close to the older TV's and you see every pixel. I didn't know what it meant or anything. I told Jeremy and explained that I didn't understand it. Our minds curious as to its meaning.

Wondrous Love

We met my parents in the kitchen at the House and had breakfast. I made pancakes, from scratch, Josh's favorites and I couldn't resist. Baking was always my release, a way to relax and let go. We ate, talked a little and then headed back to the hospital to see Josh. I couldn't wait to just kiss his little head and hold his hand.

We got in there and I went straight back. I started to talk to Josh and read to him some of the books I had downloaded on my phone. I kiss his hands and his head and run my fingers through his hair. We had brought in pictures to put up behind his bed, so we could see his smiling face and be reminded of how he was, not where he is. The nurses were kind enough to tape them up overnight.

In fact, his nurse smiled at me and said "We never get to see them before they come in here, or know who they are. Thank you for bringing them in." I smiled back and started to share a few memories of Josh. Things he liked and his personality, stuff that you would never have guessed by looking at him.

Jeremy's mom came back and we prayed together over Josh. Her on one side and me on the other, our hands joined across and over him, we prayed. Tears running down our faces, we still prayed. Our hearts lifted together for this precious life, my son, her grandson.

It was just after lunch when two unexpected visitors arrived to check in on Josh and to meet Jeremy and me. These two gentlemen came up to Jeremy and I and asked if we were Josh's parents.

"Yes, we are." Jeremy answered them.

"I'm Josh and this is Adam. We are two of the EMT's that answered the call about your son."

I started to cry and hugged them both. Jeremy and I began thanking them.

"Have you had the chance to go back to see him yet?" Jeremy asked.

"Yes, we were just back there. We left him a stuffed Mickey. We were reading your posts and about how much he liked Mickey Mouse and everything."

Tears started to well in my eyes as I smiled at them.

"I can't thank you enough that you were there."

"Well, I was actually off that day." Josh started to tell us. "My daughter was playing with my radio, which she has never touched before, when I heard the call come in about your son. We take all calls seriously but pediatric calls we step up even more for. Thankfully I live right down the road in New Cumberland."

I was amazed. The Lord had made sure that people who needed to be there were. That all the help we needed was going to be there when we needed it. We spoke for a few minutes longer and then they had to be going. We thanked them again and I hugged them both. I was in awe of what God had done, how he made sure we had help when we needed it.

"God is our refuge and strength,
A very present help in trouble."
 - Psalm 46:1

Posted Feb 25, 2011 5:53pm

"Well, today the rewarming process began. At first, they were warming Josh faster than usual, as there was no response coming from him. They started doing 1 degree Celsius per 2-3 hours. When he reached roughly 33.5°C, he began to show some reactions again. The "ripple" in his pupil returned, though slightly less than before. The reaction from the shoulder pinch that existed yesterday is gone, but in its place is a small reaction when his palm is tickled. We're unable to say for sure if this new reaction is a spinal reaction or a brain reaction.

Since we've seen at least some reaction, they are slowing the warming process down to a normal pace. Josh will be warmed at 1°C per 12 hours until he reaches a normal temp of 37°C. He is currently around 33.8°C, so it should be about 36 hours until he reaches a normal temperature. Hopefully, as his temperature increases, so too will his reactions.

The one hopeful reaction that we've seen hasn't yet been repeated. They changed Josh's diaper today while Cynthia, my mother, and myself were present. When they were cleaning Josh, his hand made a slight movement of probably about a half inch, as if he were moving his hand to push away the nurse's. Only Cynthia and my mother saw the movement. I had both of them in front of me, so I didn't see it. The nurse didn't see it ei-

Wondrous Love

ther, and the doctors weren't around at the time. We mentioned this to Dr. Bob when we had a sit-down meeting with him. He said that he (obviously) can't confirm anything, but this would seem to be a brain reaction rather than spinal, as it involved reaction to stimulation in a completely different area.

This new movement is a glimmer of hope, but hasn't been repeated or accompanied by any other new reactions. It's something new, but we're not really sure how excited to be about it. While Cynthia and I were in the room, they did a breath test. Unfortunately, his brain did not tell him to take a breath while the ventilator was turned down. They did a blood gas during the test. Josh's CO2 reached "51". At "60", a brain should certainly tell a body to breathe to expel carbon dioxide. Dr. Bob didn't want to push the test too far, but it appears that Josh is not ready to breathe on his own. As I said before, hopefully as he becomes warmer, he will offer up some new reactions.

Every time I check this site, I see more people that have signed up and new messages left by all of you. Thank you so much, yet again, for going through this with us and helping to give us strength. We really can't express how much the emotional (and edible) support means to us. A special thank you to Joshua and Adam for stopping by. They are two of the EMTs who responded to the 911 call. I want them (and all the other volunteer emergency responders) to know that they are greatly appreciated. The follow-up visit just reinforces how much they truly care about the people they help.

Here's hoping for more positive signs in the days to come. Thank you all for the continued support.

-- Jeremy"

Shortly after Jeremy made the above post, many of my friends from a Mom's Group Josh and I had joined for us to meet people, arrived with food. Lots of food. We ate well and the girls brought plenty that we had more than enough to share with others who were sitting around the family room. We just set the leftovers out on the table with a sign that read "Help yourself".

We stayed late at the hospital. We were waiting on Ben, a close friend of Jeremy's, and his wife to arrive. They were bringing oil to anoint Joshua's head. They said they were lucky and were able to get a hold of a cotton swab that had oil from a Catholic icon. It had recently been in the area and Ben was able to get a swab from it and a print out of the prayer. So with that, Ben anointed Josh's brow and said the prayer over him.

Afterwards Jeremy, Ben and Lisa went and talked for a bit, while I lingered with Josh and helped to bathe him. It felt amaz-

Cynthia Complese

ing to be able to help clean him and get him ready for bed. We washed his hair, careful to not remove the anointing oil, and washed his body. Then we put lotion on him and clean sheets and clean clothes. I rolled him close to me and held him against my chest as they moved the sheet out from under him. The smell of him and the feel of his body against me. Reminded me so much of how I missed being mom. How I missed being able to hold him and cradle him, hug and snuggle him. Even just the smell of him being near, things I missed dearly.

2
Moving Forward

Posted Feb 26, 2011 1:02am

"*I cannot say enough about the staff around Joshua. They are amazing people and in doing what they do we love them for it. Tonight's RN (Jen) was great in working with us for everything. We had a wonderful friend say a prayer over Josh and anoint him with oil.*

On top of all that, I got to help bathe my son. Yes, I got to help be a mother. You know, that thing that I have been doing for the past 2 1/2 years and am now going through withdrawals of. I can't explain how giddy I was to just help put a diaper on him and rub him down with lotion. Not to mention change his sheets and wipe his bum. I could not thank her enough and told her, "Put me to use, make me feel useful when I am back here." and she chuckled at me. I had to explain to her that I was not kidding. If you would like me to hold something, read you a number or put Vaseline on his lips, yes I would LOVE to. There is no question of would I like to, I WILL LOVE to!

In more serious notes, the warming procedure is officially half a degree every 6 hours. We are still seeing his arms twitch and I was informed tonight, that his pupil ripple is sluggish. But that it was what it was earlier today. When I said good night to him, they were preparing to hang blood for him, as his platelets were lower than we would like to see. Jen said she would look into getting information to us about donating, so if we would like to, we can donate and they can use blood we have donated first. If we would like. As I understand Josh does not have a rare blood type, but hopefully I will remember to ask his nurse tomorrow what type he does have.

I promise to try to update more, as I know so many of you are checking so often. I know there are times where we are just backing away and trying to breath. So please hang with us on the updates and we are getting them out as we can handle it. We are thankful to all of you for your prayers and kind words. Tonight is the strongest I have felt in days, and being with Joshua this evening and helping take care of him has built up strength in me I did not know I had on reserve.

Love to all! Cynthia and Jeremy"

We rose early after another late night like we had before. Breakfast in the Ronald McDonald House, my parents joined us, then we headed over to the Hospital. I handed the laptop case to Jeremy as he headed into the family area and I went headed back to Josh's room. I kissed him good morning and ran my fingers through his hair. Jeremy and I checked in with Josh's nurse. We found out that things had regressed over night, but they felt it would be best to wait for Josh's doctor to do his rounds and then speak with us. So, we waited patiently, during the wait I took that time to head down to the chapel. I needed to be in a quiet place where I could just let my mind clear and my heart cry. I sat on the floor cross legged and Jeremy sat in a chair across from me. I just had to be as low as I could. I rested me hands on my knees, took a deep breath in and closed my eyes as I exhaled.

While my eyes were closed and I was clearing my mind Josh came to me and stood in my lap. Though I knew he was not there I could feel the weight of him in my lap, like if I opened my eyes I would expect to see him there. Although my arms did not move I felt my spiritual arms reach up and wrap around him and hug him close. I could smell him as I inhaled. Then as I felt his love for me, I saw an angel place its hands on the sides of his body and hand him up to heaven. I watched as the hands of Jesus receive him. At the time, I believed it meant he needed more time, I told Jeremy "He just needs more time." While I still surged with hope, I saw hope in Jeremy's eyes fade. I didn't want to give up, not yet.

We spoke a little more as we headed upstairs, back to the family rooms and where our parents were. My mom and dad were talking about lunch plans. Mom wanted Chinese so we started to search the web for a place that would deliver to the hospital. When Josh's doctor called us back to speak about Josh's progress. It was a little after 11am by this point and we weren't sure what we were going to hear.

Posted Feb 26, 2011 12:42pm
Faith and Love

Today we came in to change. Some of it is good and some of it is a step back. Josh's pupils are not responding to light now. We do not have the ripple now. Also, when his palm is stroked, his arms do not react anymore. So, in those areas we have re-

Wondrous Love

gressed, but his fingers are showing response to painful stimulus, which that is new positive change.

Today I am feeling thin. The step back is not what we wanted but I am still praying. This afternoon I am reaching a point of numb. I am praying for strength and guidance right now. As I am not who I was yesterday. I am not who I was Thursday. The weekend has come and with it I feel deflated.

We continue to praise the lord and call upon him to heal Josh. We are continuing to call for a full recovery and for the Lord to continue to give us signs that Josh is fighting along our side. Praise you Lord for your gifts and all that you have done!

When we received the news, we asked the Doctor if he would meet with our family, so they could explain everything better to them. First hand was always better than second. He agreed and said he would meet with us shortly. About 45 minutes later we were all walking back to a small room in the NICU where we could all sit and speak. My parents were there, Jeremy's parents were there and I put my sister on speaker phone. The doctor, his assistant and Josh's nurse were all there and answered every question everyone had. I was in awe at how patient they were with everyone.

The warming process continued, but the wanted response did not come back. We were dreading what our eyes were telling us. My heart could not give up on my son, I continued to pray at his bed side. It was on this amazing day that I remember the most heart felt prayer I ever gave. I was holding his little hand in mine, I was crying over him and praying for God to heal his brain. My lips were silenced as I just looked at him. How still his body was, how fragile and delicate he was, I just stared at him and I felt my heart reach through my mouth, and for the first time I heard the words of my heart cry out.

"Father, whether he stays or he goes, I will always love you." I spoke in the softest of a whisper, tears flowing down my cheeks, my eyes on the sleep-like face of my son. The feel of his hand in mine and the mild warmth coming from him. It was in that moment, I gave my heart to God and promised to love him, no matter what.

My son, give me your heart,
And let your eyes observe my ways. - Proverbs 23:26

The day passed on and the next morning came. From the Ronald McDonald house, I made the following post, while waiting on my parents to arrive. Today we knew they were going to per-

Cynthia Complese

form an official examination and determinations would be made, this was day 6. My heart was heavy, my expectations were unknown.

Posted Feb 27, 2011 7:27am
Love and pray

Love and pray, these are thoughts that are going through my mind every second. How much I love my son, my husband, our parents, our friends, our family. How much our love for Josh has brought so many closer to us and closer to God. Things happen for a reason, in my mind God has made the choice for this to happen because many who were on the line of faith needed to be pushed over. There are things that need to happen and those of us who needed to be closer to Christ for them to happen, need to be strong in Faith. I know Christ did not do this to Josh because of anything "evil", I know it is in Love that things happen through Our Father and His Son. I also know that it happened to us, because God knew we were strong enough to do this. To stay by his side and not falter.

Today Josh will reach 37 degrees Celsius. We do not know what will happen and we know it will take a long time for Josh's brain to heal. I do not expect any of this to happen overnight. I am not expecting a fast recovery, but I do know in my heart, God will heal Josh. Josh will recover!

Then number 7 seems to be Josh's lucky number. When he was born he was 7 pounds 7 ounces. He was born 7-14-08. It took him 7 days to warm up to daycare. 7 has always been something of meaning to him. Tuesday, will be 7 days. Something in my heart tells me Tuesday will be more change. I am not expecting more until then, but I will welcome whatever change Josh has the strength to give us.

God has blessed me with sight in these times. Things have been shown to me, in times when I need them the most, so that I will not falter. Yesterday, I went to the Chapel and meditated. I knew I needed to clear my mind, as I was in a horrible funk. In there, God brought Josh's spirit to me and I felt him in my lap. I felt my spiritual arms wrap around him and I felt his cheek touch mine. Then I saw an angel, take Josh in his arms and hand him up to Christ. I know Josh is with us when we need him and I know he is with Christ when he needs to be renewed. I know that Josh must be strong in spirit so that he can fight. I know Heaven is the most beautiful place and I am sure Josh is happy there and that God is making sure he is well taken care of. Which is why I am able to take care of myself, because I know Josh is

Wondrous Love

well cared for by the hospital and that his spirit is cared for by Christ.

Had I known then what I know now, as I write these pages, I would have known that God does not create bad for us. I would have said that it was not at the hand of God that any of this happened. But I was living with a carnal mindset. At the time, I did not know God, who He was or that He was for me. I had this idea of God just standing by while life dealt cards, which I learned after communing with God and reading His Word, that is not the truth.

And you shall know the truth,
and the truth shall make you free. - John 8:32

The thief does not come except to steal, and to kill, and to destroy. I have come that they may have life, and that they may have it more abundantly. - John 10:10

We arrived to the Hospital with no change. They told us they did want to do the exam, and it would be later that afternoon. I turned to Jeremy and said, "I want to flood the prayer lines for Josh." So, we held a prayer vigil.

Posted Feb 27, 2011 12:04pm
3PM Prayer Vigil

To anyone who is reading this and interested, at 3PM today we are meeting in the hospital chapel to hold a prayer vigil for Joshua. All are welcome to come and be a part, regardless of your religious belief. We understand if you can't make it for any reason, and we thank those who are able to attend. If you're not able to make it due to distance or any other reason, please take a moment around 3PM (Eastern Time) to say a quick prayer or have a moment of reflection for Josh.
Thanks and God bless.

We took turns praying for Josh. There was a handful of us that could be there for this, but there were family and friends praying and interceding during this time. We prayed from 3pm until 4pm. I started off and our family took turns lifting prayers for Josh as we were all in agreement with each other. The moment we were gathered there was so soft and amazing. The presence of God was like a soft feather on our hearts.

Cynthia Complese

After the prayers, we went to the cafeteria where we shared goofy stories of things Josh used to say or do. Memories we could never forget because they imprinted on our lives so heavily. We shared laughter and tears, at moments laughing to the point of tears. We had amazing fellowship.

The time had come though. It was 4:45pm and Jeremy and I were asked to be present during Josh's exam, so that explanations would be easier. Jeremy took my hand in his and we took the long walk up to the PICU. The walk was slow, almost painful. The unknown racing through my mind. We arrived at the double doors into the PICU. Jeremy pressed the call button and they let us back. We put on the gown coverings they requested of us each time entering the PICU and they had placed two chairs at Josh's bedside, for Jeremy and I. The curtain was pulled and there at Josh's bed was his nurse, his doctor and his doctor's aide. The exam was ready to begin. I took a breath and my heart began to cry out to God as I watched them test for different brain reflexes.

They shined a light in his right eye, his pupil didn't respond. They shined a light in his left eye, his pupil didn't respond. They pinched his shoulder, but his body didn't react. They waited a moment and watched for any reaction, they tried again, still nothing. They pinched his cuticle, no pain reflex. They tried again, still nothing. Josh's doctor looked at Jeremy and I and said "We are going to turn off the ventilator and see if his brain will trigger him to breath."

They closely monitored Josh as the ventilator was turned off, we waited... and waited. The time had passed for him to breath but the doctor wanted to wait just a moment longer and give Josh the chance. I couldn't take it. Tears streaming down my face, I climbed off the chair I was on and left the area in a hurry. Jeremy followed behind me shortly after I had left. All I could do was cry. I knew what the test meant, but I was not ready to hear it. I cried in Jeremy's arms to the point of shaking. Josh's doctor wanted to meet with us to discuss things, as was procedure.

Jeremy and I requested a room that was away from our families, because we didn't want to see them right then. They took us back into the NICU where there was conference room we could use. We sat down and went over the test. They mentioned sending someone from the Gift of Life program over to us, and we said that would be fine. They mentioned doing another test by another team in the morning, and we said ok. Then, all I could do at that moment was start to thank Josh's team. I thanked his nurse and his doctor and the aide that was there for

Wondrous Love

taking such amazing care of Josh and doing all that they could for him. I remember the look on Josh's doctor's face when he quickly said he had to go, his aide said that our words had touched his heart.

The aide and the nurse, and Josh's doctor spoke with our families in a private room. While they were in there, Jeremy and I quietly got out of there and went outside to the front of the hospital. Careful to make sure our families didn't see us. Jeremy's best friend, Chris, was in the room with our parents. Jeremy was getting text updates while we were sitting in a garden.

Looking at each other all we could say is "How are we not a wreck?" We could not understand how we were still together, how we were not puddles on the floor, from what we told via text, like our Mothers were. How were we ok?

Peace I leave with you, My peace I give to you; not as the world gives do I give to you. Let not your heart be troubled, neither let it be afraid. - John 14:27

At 9:33pm, we made this post:

Posted Feb 27, 2011 9:33pm
Bad News

Today, we received the worst news so far. This evening, around 5PM, the doctors performed an official physical exam to test for brain function. Without getting into details, this was a series of tests that should cause anyone with even the slightest brain function to react. This test is the official line between legally alive and legally dead. Joshua gave no reaction to any of the tests.

Joshua has been declared brain dead by the first set of doctors. After this, we have requested a flow scan, which will consist of a radioactive isotope being injected into Josh and a subsequent imaging of his body's blood flow. This will show if his brain if receiving any blood. We have requested this because a scan showing no blood flow would confirm brain death and reassure us that the doctors are absolutely correct.

Following this test will be another physical exam by a second set of doctors. Since declaring someone brain dead is a very difficult thing, they want two sets of doctors to come to the same conclusion before ruling it as a diagnosis. The second set of doctors is likely to be neurosurgeons, as they are experts in the brain and have already been involved, at least partly, in his case.

Cynthia Complese

If this set of doctors comes to the same conclusion, Joshua will be declared officially brain dead and life support will be removed.

Thank you all for your support so far. It has been very awe inspiring to see the amount of people that came to support us in our time of need. We are appreciative beyond explanation. We will likely ask for continued support as we move forward. Thank you for being our shoulders to cry on. Thank you for the food. Thank you for making us laugh when we needed. Thank you for just being with us. Thank you.

Jeremy and I walked the halls with my friend Heather and Jeremy's friend Chris. Just walking and talking, not sure what to say or how to react. We just needed to absorb this new "reality" We took the elevator down to the vending machines and grabbed a soda, then just walked. Standing still seemed so odd. We made our way, slowly, to the main entrance. We passed a family of four, the husband was agitated at the child in his arms and was trying to get the mother to take him, while she was fussing with a smaller child.

"If only they could know what we know" I whispered to Jeremy.

He took his hand in mine and kept walking, tears brimming in my eyes as we continued past them. Part of me wished I had spoken up and told them, but then I didn't know if I should have or not.

That night, they gave me the chance to go back and hold Josh. It was awkward and difficult, because his body was heavy and limp, but I held him in my arms, in a chair, as long as I could. When my arms were going numb and I couldn't support his weight anymore, I had to put him back in his bed. Although I didn't want to, I wanted that moment to last forever. To feel his body in my arms, forever. I didn't want to forget the sound of his laugh, the touch of his skin or smell of his hair. I didn't want to be without him.

We did hand prints and foot prints of his precious hands and feet. They had done a casting of his hand for me already before we came in.We met with the Gift of Life Organ Donor Representative at around 11pm. We immediately decided to donate whatever they could from Josh's body. Because it was H1N1 that caused the problems, there were only certain parts that could be donated. When I looked at Jeremy and said "I wonder if Tyler needs a heart?" I immediately called my best friend, and the mother of my son's best friend, Tyler.

Wondrous Love

"Courtney, I am sorry I am calling so late."

"No, it's ok, what's up?"

"Well, we are meeting with Gift of Life, and I am calling to see if Tyler is on a transplant list for his heart."

The conversation in memory is a bit disoriented beyond that, but it turned out Tyler was not on a list for a new heart. So, we told the representative that it would be fine to donate as needed.

It was nearly 2am by the time we left, the night was a warmer gorgeous night, for February. Jeremy and I got out to the car and we realized I forgot the laptop in the family room. So, we went together and walked back up to the family room, a slow and steady walk. I quietly went in the family room and got it off a counter and walked back out to Jeremy. We walked down the halls, toward the exit. Passing several people on the way, wondering to myself "Who can tell that we lost someone". When we got into our room at the Ronald McDonald House, Jeremy and I realized I left our phone charger in the family room as well. Knowing we needed it, we looked at each other and decided neither of us wanted to go, so we both went. We walked slowly and sluggishly up to the family room and got it. Then we walked back slowly back out to the car, a lot slower than the first 2 times we had left the hospital. I was starting to cry a little, what water I had left in my system at this point. Tears slowly went down my cheeks, no sobbing, just a stream. I could feel my heart aching. When we reached the front doors, it was starting to rain. I gave a solemn chuckle and looked at Jeremy.

"It's said, *'When you cry, God cries with you'*." I spoke, looking at the rain slowly falling, like subtle tears.

As soon as the last word left my lips, the skies opened and the soft rain turned into a heavy down pour. It was in that moment, that I began to realize. It is not God's will for children to die, God did not want us hurting.

You see, the night of the 27th, Jeremy and I laid in bed at the Ronald McDonald House, where we took turns crying and lifting each other up. At one point, I had just stopped crying, when Jeremy played a song that Chris posted on Facebook. Tears in Heaven, by Eric Clapton. I had never known the story, so Jeremy shared it with me briefly and we listened to the words. It was at the end of this song that Jeremy started to cry.

"It isn't fair" he began

"I know" I whispered, my arm around him trying to comfort him.

"You've seen Josh and my mom has, but I haven't." tears started to flow and I was watching my strong watchtower break. His eyes closed and tears fell freely. When he opened his eyes, he looked at me and said, "I just saw him..." Tears flowed again, when they calmed once more he began again. "I saw him, he was on my Nan's lap." It was the site that would be most comforting to him. I knew this was what he needed.

The next day passed quickly. We met at the hospital around 9am. A friend brought donuts and bagels, we talked and waited for the final results. Then they came. After being back at the Ronald McDonald House, for our last night there and after visiting with some friends that came out to be with us. We made this post.

Joshua Has Passed
Posted Feb 28, 2011 7:09pm

Joshua's second exam was negative, just as the first test was. There was no visible brain activity. For peace of mind, we requested a flow scan also. The flow scan showed no blood flow to Joshua's brain. This gave us a little extra confirmation that the doctors are correct. With the two exams and flow scan all being negative, Josh has been declared brain dead and officially pronounced dead.

I'm not sure what else to add to this update. I'm sure CC will add another with more. I don't know if any of them will read this, but I want to thank the staff at Hershey Medical Center's PICU, specifically Dr. Bob, Dr. Melissa, and his nurses (Sarah, Jen, Margo, Jake, Cara, and Katie). All were extremely caring for Josh's medical condition, as well as the emotional condition of both of us, as well as our entire group of friends and family. There are not enough words to say how helpful these people have been this far into our grieving period.

I also want to thank the EMT crew that rushed to Joshua's aid when he needed all the help he could get. I especially want to thank Joshua Zeiders and Adam Smith. It's absolutely awesome people like these two that help save lives on a daily basis.

Wondrous Love

Our society could not survive without them and New Cumberland is much better for having them. Thank you for your service. Thank you for what you did for Joshua. Thank you for visiting us in the hospital.

Next, I want to thank our friends and family. We would not have been able to make it through this without all of you. We still have a long road ahead of us, but with all of you to help support us, I'm sure we can make it. We love you all and thank you for the shoulders to cry on, food, and laughter when we need it.

Finally, I want to thank Joshua. I think that Joshua has made me a better man, husband, and father. I pray that one day, if and when we're ready, we'll be blessed with another son. I'd love to be an even better father in the future. I don't want a replacement for Joshua. He can't be replaced. I love you, Joshua.

-- Jeremy

Edit: My initial post included all of my thanks, but none of my hopes. We have chosen to donate Joshua's organs to other children who need them. I hope that they are received and well used by children, whether local, regional, national, or international. For whatever reason, Josh had to die. I hope we can make sure that at least one other family is spared from what we are dealing with by virtue of the body that Joshua left behind.

Followed quickly by another post, with about as good of news as we could get at this point.

Finally, some form of good news
Posted Feb 28, 2011 8:19pm

We just received a call from the PICU. They were calling to let us know that they found a 100% match for Joshua's liver and kidneys. They think they've found a perfect match for the heart, as well, but they have to double check compatibility. It's nice to FINALLY hear some kind of good news.

I pray that the surgeries to implant these organs goes well. I pray that the organs suit the children who need them and that there is no problem with rejection. I pray that the children who receive the organs grow to use them wisely and have long lives. I pray that the families of those who receive the organs are comforted by the extension of life that Joshua has provided.

Here's to hoping they find more matches to more organs. It's the little bit of solace in the darkness we're currently facing.

-- Jeremy

Cynthia Complese

The first post I made that day, was a solemn one, but Jeremy and I had put much discussion and thought into this matter throughout the day. Jeremy and I both liked the idea of reflecting Josh as much as we could.

Posted Feb 28, 2011 9:41pm
In the days to come....

Hopefully, within a few days, we will know when Josh's memorial will be. There will not be a viewing.

I post this now, because I want all to know our "expectations" moving forward. Joshua was such an amazing and bright little boy, and he knew all of his colors... except black. On that note, we do NOT want black to be warn. We want to see people in bright colors and casual clothes. Anytime Josh was in a Sunday Best Attire, he would throw a fit (and we have pictures to prove it). So we want to see people laughing and celebrating his life. We aren't sure where his memorial will be. We do not know what all we have planned.... except that Josh loved colors and shapes and would point them out as we walked around places.

Jeremy and I are planning to be returning to our home tomorrow. The thought of facing the house is tough, but we know we have to do it. I cannot thank all of you enough for the thoughts, prayers and food. When we were too numb to think of our health, our friends and family did for us. Jeremy and I are thankful for that.

I have to thank my Mom's Group, which is more like a band of sisters. You ladies have become such a strong part of my life, I could not be strong today without you by my side. You ladies have laughed with me and cried with me. We have griped together and lifted each other up. I am reminded of the movie Steel Magnolias. That is sooooo us! I love you, girls!
~Cynthia

Joshua's celebration of life was set for March 5th at the LDS church in Carlisle. The days leading up to it, I was numb. We had to meet with the funeral home and make decisions for a casket and meet with the people at the cemetery to purchase his plot, so his body could be buried. We also needed to meet with someone about a headstone. Before leaving the Ronald McDonald House, that afternoon, we received word that Josh's organs had been sent to recipients. The following post was the last made at the House.

Wondrous Love

Posted Mar 1, 2011 12:05pm
His little organs

Josh's Liver and Kidneys were the only organs they could match up. Today I was told his liver went to an 8 yr old boy and was being put in as I am typing this. His kidney's will be going to two different recipients, but they do not have their information because they are not in this area.

I was told they had a match for his heart, but that his heart would be too large for the child.

We have begun arrangements for Josh. Hopefully soon we will know a definite when and where and what will be going on.

Thank you and God Bless.
Cynthia

Now it was time, we had to walk into our home without our son. It was March 1st, we walked into the house late that afternoon, thankfully greeted by our 3 cats. The sound of them in the house, made it seem not as empty. We set Josh's belongings down by the couch and placed a meal that we had just received in the fridge. Heather had come to drop it off, but decided to join us at Cracker Barrel with Chris, Ben and Lisa. I knew I didn't want to be in the house. We met them there, except for Heather, she followed us over from our place.

We needed some laughs, almost like we needed air at this point. In the presence of our amazing friends, our sorrows could escape us.

It was close to 9pm when we arrived back at our place, following a trip to the local Borders Books. They were closing and figured we'd take a minute to see if they had anything we wanted. Pretty much anything to keep us from the house and longer with company. Jeremy and I headed to the computer room to play some games straight away. We were in there a while when I realized, I had forgotten something downstairs. So, I left my computer to go down and get it. It was in the bag with Josh's things from the hospital.

My hand brushed across a fleece blanket and then a stuffed Mickey fell from the bag. It hit me then. I had not broken until that moment. Warm tears rolled down my face, like rain in the middle of summer. My knees buckled, as the realization of Josh never being in the house again struck every part of me.

I crumbled to my living room floor, sobbing. I heard Jeremy run down the steps, as I lifted my tear soaked face I saw him rushing towards me.

Cynthia Complese

"He's gone..." was all I could bare to speak in a whisper.

Jeremy lifted me to my feet and wrapped his arms around me. I buried my face in his chest and let the tears flow. With every tear that left me I felt a little more peace come over me. When the night was over, I felt prepared to face the days ahead. My sister was coming in the next day, to represent the family in the coming events. I didn't know how everything was going to look, but I felt peace.

Our first morning back at home, neither of us wanted to get out of bed. We knew we had things to get done, but lying in bed sounded better. Until I went to rollover, I couldn't move my feet. The weight of our oldest cat, Wicket, had securely pinned my feet into their current position. As I became more awake by that realization, I felt the soft weight of four paws on my chest. I opened my eyes to two bright, yellow eyes staring at me. They seemed to glow, in contrast to the black fur that surrounded them.

Thrall, who was Josh's cat, had not joined the other two in making me their personal cat bed. Instead he was seen down the hall, curled into a tight ball in front of Josh's door. We had heard him crying and meowing outside his door in the middle of the night. I moved Nel from my chest, she was very much a kitten still. I took a moment to scratch Wicket's head and smooth the fur along her side and pet Thrall a bit as I was on my way past him to the bathroom. I came back to the bedroom and roused Jeremy. We got dressed and went out for breakfast. Every part of our house reminded us of Josh, I needed to get away.

We headed out to Bob Evans for a bite and began the talk of which cemetery to use. We liked the idea of picking one near our home. Rolling Green was just down the street and would drive past it on the way to nearly anywhere. I called them and scheduled a meeting for later that afternoon. I then called the funeral home and scheduled a meeting with them for that Friday, the 4th . We went home to waste time while waiting for our noon meeting. We had invited Jeremy's mom to join us, we didn't know what we were doing and she had been through all of this with her parents. Also, we hoped it would help with the grieving process, she loved Josh as much as we did and was a strong part in his life.

I called the LDS Bishop, Jeremy and I had already decided on wanting to have Josh's celebration on Saturday. The thought to have it at the LDS church came to my mind, and figured it would be nice. Bishop Dilts finalized the date and time with us, we determined how we were doing everything and decided on

Wondrous Love

display boards with photos of Josh. I had plenty of scrapbook supplies to use to decorate with his personality. I then quickly posted the service information on his CarePage.

We made plans for the next day to pick up my sister, Liz, from Middletown airport. I knew it was going to be a hectic week, but I felt ready for it. Jeremy and I were pretty much living from one meal to the next. We didn't really plan our nights or next days, just lived moment by moment.

Noon quickly approached and Jeremy and I were on our way to Rolling Green Cemetery. Jeremy's mom met us there and the three of us headed in together. The waiting area was nicely decorated, with flowers and a stand with pamphlets on it. The counter that allowed you to speak with the secretary was wooden and also nicely decorated. On the right-hand side sat pamphlets about dealing with death and headstones.

"Hi, I'm Cynthia, we have a 12:30 appointment" I told the woman on the other side of the counter. She smiled back at me gently. I knew that it took certain people to be able to do certain jobs, this was one of those of the jobs.

"It will be just one moment, can I get you a coffee or water?" she quickly offered us.

Jeremy and his mom asked for water and I took up the offer for a cup of coffee. They showed us back to a small room with an oval table in the center and the receptionist ran off to get the drinks. On the walls hung different headstones and markers with information about them. I didn't know what to expect at this point. Large binders sat on the table and soon a woman came through the door with a clipboard and a thick Russian accent.

"Hi, I'm Renate, I am so sorry about your loss." she began, "How can we assist you?"

"Well, we just lost our 2 year old son on Monday." I began to explain.

The look in Renate's eyes showed true concern for the situation.

"There are several options," she started to explain, "because he was so young he would qualify for what is called Babyland. Where we supply a plot at no charge, but it's all depending on size."

Cynthia Complese

"He was a big boy" my mother in law, Terry said. A small smile slightly moved across my face, because he was a very big boy for his age. Josh was only 2 ½ but wore a 5T shirt and 3T pant. Many people looked at his size and thought he was 5 years old, but when you heard him talk you knew he was only 2 or 3.

Renate began to describe the size requirements for the baby area, and we knew Josh would fit the requirements, barely. She then began to describe another area of plots, where we would have the option of being buried next to him if we wanted. Something in that seemed comforting to Jeremy and I, and his parents too.

"Let me go get a map." Renate stated as she left the room.

This was perfect, we had a chance to talk things over. Renate had told us that if we wanted a plot that was not in the baby area, it was going to cost us $1,200. This was money we did not have, at least not exactly. I knew I was going to get something close to that back from Josh's daycare, because I had paid for the entire semester up front. I called the daycare and told them what was going on.

"Is there any way I could swing by and pick up the check today? I really need to be able to pay for this now." I asked the manager at the daycare.

"I don't see it being a problem. I will call the owner and get everything taken care of." They told me.

"Thank you so much!" I was elated to know that we were going to be able to bury Josh's body in a timely manner.

Renate had returned with a larger map of the area and what seemed to be blank contracts. She started to explain the layout to us and where everything was. "This is the baby area" she explained, pointing to an area of the map that was near the office, "and these are the plots I was telling you about, that are the buy one plot get another plot free." She started to point to the area near a statue of Jesus kneeling, near the main entrance.

"I used to take Josh to that area, around July 4th and Memorial Day, he loved to see the flags." I told Jeremy, but loud enough that everyone could here.

Wondrous Love

"Yes, this is lane that we line with American Flags during that time."

"I know..." I said quietly, thinking back to when Josh and I would drive through there and look at the flags. It had taken no time, really, to take a slight detour and drive through the cemetery so Josh could see the flags when we were headed anywhere. "Fah!" I could hear Josh, in the back seat, pointing at the flags and exclaimed random noises. He spoke his own language, we used to call it 'Joshese'. I remember being fluent in it.

"I think we are going to go with one of those plots" Jeremy began to tell Renate, which brought me out of my daydream, "we would like a plot where Cynthia and I can purchase two next to him."

"We want to purchase two by him, as well" Terry had piped in.

I started to cry at the thought that we were picking our burial plots already, but only because we had to pick Josh's plot. Renate began writing up two contracts for us and one for Jeremy's mom. The plots that were for us and Jeremy's parents, were on a payment plan. However, we needed to pay for Josh's plot completely and upfront. Thankfully, Terry brought her checkbook, while none of us had that much cash, she wrote the check to them and we were going to transfer the money to her account from the check we got from the daycare.

Jeremy and I were thankful that we had life insurance on Josh. It's not something a parent thinks about, but I remember Jeremy saying it was only 65 cents a pay, well worth it now that we had to face this.

"There are a few options," Renate began pointing at different plots that had 5 in a row, which would meet our requests.

"Let's do this one" I said, pointing to a row of plots that were right along the roadside. "This will put him right by the flags when they are up." That thought seemed warming to my heart, that he would be near something he loved, it seemed an appropriate way to honor him.

"No problem." Renate wrote up the contracts and we gave her the check and got everything squared away.

Cynthia Complese

Our next stop was Josh's daycare. We needed to get that check deposited right away. The code for the door slid off my fingers like I was dropping Josh off yesterday. I didn't even think about the numbers as I punched them in. I heard the door click and the electric lock unlatched. Jeremy opened the door and I slowly stepped in, the familiar smell wafted through the entrance and I half expected Josh to chatter with excitement. I glanced at Jeremy and he smiled at me gently. The manager, Wendy, saw us from a distance and came right over. Several of the teachers there saw us as well, you could see the pang of sadness on their faces at just the sight of us being there. The hallway was brightly colored with the children's art work hung on the walls, it was March and the Valentine's decorations were coming down and some St. Patrick's Day decorations were already up. The normally cheerful hallway seemed a bit dull and sad.

"You could have called and I would have run it out, you didn't need to come in." She said as she handed me an envelope. "Did you get Josh's things? Someone had come by and picked them up for you." She informed us.

"Not yet, but they did let us know they had them, thank you." I had responded. "We wanted to let you know that Josh's services will be this Saturday the 5th."

"We saw, thank you so much, we didn't know what we were going to do if it would have been on a weekday." True concern was on her face. "I won't personally be able to stay long, I have a family thing I need to be at, but I will stop in for a bit."

"That's totally fine, we understand. Thank you." I smiled at her weakly and she gently smiled back.

Jeremy and I headed back to the car, knowing this was probably the last time I would be in this building.

From there we went straight to the ATM and deposited the check into Jeremy's account. Then we went off to Rite Aid. I had a thumb drive with hundreds of photos of Josh on it and I needed prints.

"Tomorrow night we are meeting at Krista's house so that the Mom's Group can help me put these together" I was telling Jeremy and we were going through picking out photo after photo of Josh. After we had decided to print all of them but 6, we were ready to submit the request. When I saw the cost I was shocked, "It's almost $100..." I whispered to Jeremy.

Wondrous Love

"It's ok, it's Josh." Jeremy reassured me with half a smile and an arm around my back, as he hit the submit button on the photo machine. I smiled back at him. I was ready to go home and do something that involved me not thinking. We ordered pizza that night and spent the evening playing video games, online with our friends. All I kept focusing on was getting through this. Getting through his burial and these plans. Tomorrow we meet with the funeral home and we pick my sister up at the airport, I also had to figure out how to fit all these photos onto 6 tri-fold boards to tell Josh's life. Thankfully I was going to have about 12 great friend helping me with that. But right now, I could relax, stop thinking and just play a video game with my husband and friends. I could breathe.

Morning of the 3rd came quickly and I woke Jeremy around 11am. We needed to set things in order, I needed to get my sister from the airport and pick up the photos from Rite Aid. Thankfully Jeremy's parents opened their home to my sister, so she could stay there. We left the house around 1pm, thankful for the cats in our home to make us laugh. One of them was still a kitten and she has the impeccable ability to do something silly at the perfect moment, when you need a laugh.

We grabbed a bite to eat at a diner and went to Rite Aid to pick up the photos. The stack was enormous and I was excited to look at every photo. Although that would have to wait until I got home, I didn't want to risk dropping any of them. Jeremy and I stopped at Michael's and he put up with me searching through the store for ideas. How his love for me had grown in this time. Our respect for each other was higher than I had ever thought it would be. When we left the Hospital the first thing we were told was that we needed to be prepared. When we asked for what, they proceeded to inform us that most marriages end in divorce after losing a child. I remember I had looked at Jeremy and smiled, holding his hand tight. I was not going to let that happen.

It was getting close to the time we needed to be at the airport. So, we stopped at Jeremy's mom's house, and swapped cars. Her car allowed for more comfortable seating then our little sedan. Then off we left for the airport. I was nervous but excited. I hadn't seen my sister in years and I was thankful for her to come out. We parked mom's car and headed toward the covered walkways. The moving walkways were fun and I was playing on one as we went. It felt good to laugh.

We stepped out of the walkway into a small area that had escalators the took you straight into the lobby. The lobby of the airport was comfortably lined with rocking chairs and the center

Cynthia Complese

of the airport had a design on the floor of the Pennsylvania seal that had star points coming off of it. Each point had a picture on it that was part of their history. While I wasn't from there I felt a strong connection to the state. This was my home.

We waited Liz to arrive. I was nervous and I talked about everything I could. Jeremy would chuckle and smile at me, letting me know I was rambling. I would smile back and hug into him. Our marriage wasn't perfect, but it was us. We checked Liz's flight on the board and it showed the status as arrived. I got excited and made my way to the side of the lobby where passengers would be exiting. I knew she would be there any minute. Sure enough, I saw her blond hair and knew right away, that was my sister.

She walked passed the security and I gave her a big smile and an even bigger hug. It felt good to have family near again. Mom and dad had only been gone from us two days and here was my sister now. I still wished, deep down, that my parents could have stayed. While thankful for them being there through the hospital time, I still missed them.

We gathered Liz's luggage from the turnabout down stairs. Got back to the car, paid for parking and headed out of Harrisburg Airport. I wanted to show Liz so much while she was here, because I knew she was a huge Civil War buff. At the same time, I knew why she was here, and all that would have to wait. We stopped for dinner on the way back to Lemoyne, where Terry and Jerry (Jeremy's parents) lived. We swapped out cars and let Liz get situated, before rushing her off with me to drop off Jeremy and go build the displays. I had packed card stock, cutters and stamps, ways to customize all the amazing moments we had with Josh.

I had purchased 6 display boards and printed out Josh's name nicely. I had pictures of his life, in a stack in an envelope. Stickers that portrayed events but also his favorite things, sat in a bag next to the card stock. As he got out of the car at Krista's house, and headed up the driveway. Some people had already arrived and some were still coming in. It was a great time and full of laughter. Liz helped to keep us on track, as many of us would get side tracked and talk the night away otherwise. She helped us to keep our eyes on the goal at hand.

The first board was done. It was bright blue with Josh's name in dark blue on white paper with a light blue border. His favorite color. Pictures of his birth and the first few months of his life precisely placed. Stickers that read "my son", "angel" and "love" placed near his precious photos. The second board, it's vibrant green being the key to the photos placed. All the amazing

Wondrous Love

out door shots of Josh were selected for this one. With full sheets of blue, neon green, orange and yellow placed randomly as a contrasting color, decorated with star stickers throughout.

Stories and memories began to scatter the living room, dining room, and kitchen. Each photo began a new story. Our tracks of mind were spilling off, as we finished the third board of bright yellow. Liz reeled us back in as we started on the red board. This was Josh's Christmas's, primarily. At the bottom of the center portion I place 3 pictures, one of each visit to Santa from each year. Tears began to swell as I remembered taking him to the first visit. How unprepared we were. His clothes were not Christmas and it was so last minute. Terry and had met us there, and thankfully she had clothes that were the season. While his socks were still a baby blue, his jumper was evergreen. He did well with Santa, no screaming or crying. In fact, his look was rather peaceful. Santa had to keep pulling his hands from his mouth for the photos, but the pictures were nice.

The stories continued and I trailed off often as time went by. Soon we had one board left and people were starting to trickle out. This last one had to get done. Liz, Krista, Allie and I worked on it. The last of a crew of 12 that were still able to focus on the task at hand. Which was so like our group. This last board was his last birthday, and family photos. Those precious moments that we never wanted to slip by. Pictures of Josh and his daddy, Josh with his Grammy and with Pop Pop. Our first family photo, seconds after he was born. The moment when my life changed forever, when he was in my arms. Pictures from his first birthday were set to the left panel and the family photos to the right. His second birthday filled the center. This was how I wanted to remember him. The laughter, the giggles, the silly language, and the joy he filled me with. Not one photo was taken while he laid in the hospital bed, so he can never be remembered for how he left, but only for who he was.

We finished the board, tears wiped away and resting on tissues. Liz and I closed them up and set them by the door with the leftover supplies I had. I was happy it was done and ready for part two. Tomorrow we meet with the funeral home about Josh's casket, but for now. I was with friends and family, enjoying their company. For tomorrow, the pain would start fresh, but for now, I can laugh.

I woke the next morning, my arm around Jeremy and a cat on my pillow. My eyes opened slowly and I realized my surroundings. I got up and went to the bathroom. Josh's bedroom door was still closed. It was alien to me, to look as his shut door and know that he wasn't in there playing, waiting for us to come

Cynthia Complese

get him. Knowing that he was going to shout over the monitor or knock his door, letting us know it was time to get up. It was a foreign feeling, as my hand touched the cold metal doorknob and I thought to open it. My hand moved from the door knob to the center of the door, a tear escaped my eye as I whispered "I love you" and walked back to bed. It was 8am, about the time Josh would normally wake me. I wasn't ready to face the day. I curled up next to Jeremy again and went back to sleep.

By 11am Jeremy and I were both ready to face the day. We were meeting with the funeral home today. Time seemed to drag leading up to meetings, but then speed past while the meeting took place. My mother in law drove over with my sister, while Jeremy and I met them at the funeral home. We walked in the door, it was beautiful inside. We were greeted by a tall gentleman in a suit.

"Hi, Mrs. Complese?" He asked.

"Yes," I replied, reaching to shake his out stretched hand.

"I'm Steve"

"This is my husband Jeremy, his mom Terry and my sister Liz."

"Nice to meet you." he spoke as he shook everyone's hand. "If you'll follow me back this way." He ushered us down a hallway into a large room with an equally proportionate table in the center. On the table were catalogs, books, and binders. The walls had headstones and garments for burial on them. While the sense of death was in the room, it did not smell of death. It was a fresh smell in the air and it was rather soothing. "Can I get you some water or coffee?" We all accepted the offer of water. He left the room to get the requests.

"This is who we used for Nan and Pap's funerals" Terry began to explain. Nan and Pap were her parents.

The meeting started off awkwardly. We all knew why we were there, but putting it nicely was not always easiest when dealing with a small child.

"The beginning of this book here," he said, laying a catalog in front of us, "will have the baby and small child accommodations in it."

Wondrous Love

I opened the book and began to look at some of them. "What if we wanted something else?" I had asked, having in mind something with more color to it.

"You would be looking at an adult size casket and you would need a burial vault with that. State requires that they be used in burials. I would recommend the baby rest casket, it has the vault built in, so that would not need to purchase one." he turned the catalog to the page with the baby rest casket. It was white with long rails on the side, that looked like handles. I looked to Jeremy, his mom, and my sister for thoughts. Jeremy in turn looked to his mom.

"Will he fit in the baby rest? He is a big boy." Terry asked the gentleman.

"I know, I saw him. I think he would fit in the larger size." Steve responded to her.

"I don't know.." I began, thoughts not really coming to me.

Terry and my sister both reinstated that the decision was ours to make. I looked to Jeremy, he gave a subtle nod and I returned it. "We'll do the baby rest."

"okay," Steve took a few notes and looked back to us "how many death certificates will you need?"

I turned to Jeremy. I had not even thought about that. "We'll need one for the Life Insurance" he said.

"And one for our records" I added "maybe one for my parents and one for yours, for genealogy purposes."

"I think 6 will be fine." We decided, and that was it. We signed some paperwork and worked some final details about what would be needed for the next day.

"I'll meet you there tomorrow, with a guest book and some cards." Steve informed us, and with that the meeting was over. We walked out to the parking lot and started to talk about where to go for lunch.

Cynthia Complese

"How about Isaac's?" I asked, I wanted to show my sister some new places out here. Everyone agreed quickly, after an explanation to my sister of what Isaac's is. A calm lunch there and then Liz and I took a trip to store to get provisions for tomorrow. The thoughts of the next day made me nervous. Tomorrow was Josh's service, his celebration of life. We had planned to arrive early and get things set up. I had some frames for pictures of Josh to be in, was a 8x10 photo I had taken for my Black and White photography class, that I loved the look on his face in.

The evening was rather sluggish and I was ready for bed earlier than previous nights. Our house was stocked with paper products for the next day and we had asked everyone to bring food, to help with the event. Things sat piled next to the front door, ready to load up in the morning. I had set out the blue shirt my mom had bought me while she was here. My favorite color was always purple, but blue was quickly catching up. Josh's favorite color, and I was ready to find any reason to wear it. Our clothes for the next day were set aside and ready, everything was together at the door. I did a quick once over and was ready to get some sleep. The next day was going to need a whole new reserve of energy.

I woke up early, around 8am, and went straight for the shower. I felt numb by this point. I washed my hair and scrubbed my face, my eyes burning from either lack of sleep or all the tears I'd shed, maybe both. I dried off, standing in the tub as Wicket, our cat pushed the door open and walked in. I took a sharp gasp as the cold air from the hallway rushed in, so much for the room being warm. She looked at me and went off to drink from the water fountain they had at the sink.

I finished drying off and brushed my hair out. Looking in the mirror at my face, my hair and my puffy eyes. I realized I didn't recognize the person I was looking at anymore. For the past two years spending time in front of a mirror was a luxury and makeup even more so. I slowly gathered my hair to just below the crown of my head. My mind went to how Josh used to fling my hair and didn't recognize me when I had cut it all off. It took a few hours before he would look at me. It was growing back now, I always liked it better long even though it took more time. It was just barely long enough to throw into a ponytail.

I tied it back with a blue hair tie and went to wake Jeremy. I looked at the clock and it was a little after 10, I had not realized how long I had spent in the shower, but it felt good. I snuggled up to Jeremy and he snuggled back. We hadn't touched this much in a long time. Our marriage had become one of chores and "honey do", not so much of discussions and love. I was

Wondrous Love

thankful at that moment that we had overcome our obstacle in August of last year.

I laid there, my right arm over him, thinking about that time. We were at Ben and Lisa's Wedding when we fell in love again. How he held me and danced with me. Before that day, we were talking about getting divorced. Neither of us was happy and we found more times we fought than laughed. Something had to give, and we were both talking about quitting. It was that day, when Jeremy and I danced in each other's arms and laughed, that we realized we loved each other still, we just had not paused long enough to see it. We left late that evening from their wedding and made plans for counseling. Along with the counseling and setting aside "date night" every week, our marriage was growing. We made time for us, today I was thankful we had. There was a sense of peace and comfort when he wrapped me in his arms.

As my thoughts crossed that, he stretched and rolled over, wrapping me in his arms. I cried. How I love him and I was broken. He held me, and I cried.

It was noon when we arrived at the church. I had composed myself pretty quickly and Jeremy and I got things together and made our way there. I went to the front doors and they were locked. I looked around outside, the signs of snow were gone and it was warmer out. Warm enough I wasn't wearing a jacket. I stood at the front doors, looking to see if there was anyone to let us in, when the door behind me opened and I jumped. There in the doorway was the bishop with a smile.

He welcomed us in and unlocked the doors. He showed us to the social hall, where the tables were set up and we discussed a little bit of the layout. We had decided to place the display boards on the stage and a station at the end of the stage for people to write down memories that they were willing to share. There were 3 displays of flowers that had been delivered in honor of Josh. We lined them up with the board displays. It looked beautiful. I had brought in some pictures from the walls at home and set those up at the end by the memory area.

Steve arrived from the funeral home with the Guest Book and thank you cards. "Are you sure you don't need us?" he had asked me.

"No, I think we'll be ok. Thank you." I responded, shaking his hand. He smiled back and headed out.

We placed the Guest Book on a small podium by the sanctuary with it was a black and white 8x10 of Josh I had taken, and

Cynthia Complese

then 2 wallet photos in frames that matched the 8x10. One was of just Josh from his first birthday and the other was one of a handful of photos of Josh and I. There weren't many, but because of that there were plenty of him.

People started to arrive and I began greeting as I could. We talked and laughed, some of us cried together. Soon it was time to go in and be seated in the sanctuary. The bishop spoke about salvation and gently touched a few things he could imagine, like Josh as a young adult in Heaven. Three of the young woman from the church got up, one of them sang while another played the violin and the third the piano. They played Families Can Be Together Forever, following that Chris, Jeremy's friend stood up and sang On Eagles Wings with piano accompaniment. It was beautiful, Chris did amazing. During the songs and even as the bishop would speak, some of the babies in the room would start to talk. It made me smile a little. That was Josh, he was never one to just sit still.

The bishop closed with prayer and invited everyone back to the social hall. We slowly walked out of the room and made our way back. Talking about Josh the whole way. Several introductions were made along the way. One of our friends from the bowling alley had come up to us, as she did Terry and I were talking about how Josh was there and that he was "riling" up the kids.

"He had to be!" She piped in, "my daughter was talking loud a lot and she doesn't do that, she is very shy."

I gave a small chuckle, it was so like Josh. The EMT's, Josh and Adam, had made it out. So, we introduced them to Terry and she in turn made more introductions. My sister had the chance to meet a lot of people there and soon we were sitting in the social hall.

"Have you eaten yet?" Liz asked me at one point.

"Not yet, I'll get there." I nodded to her.

"I can get you a plate, I'm heading up. Anything you would like?"

"I'm not picky." I had smiled to her. I wasn't all that hungry, but it was my family and our friends that made sure we took care of ourselves. Jeremy followed behind Liz and grabbed some

Wondrous Love

food. We sat down and tried to eat. It was almost every two bites that someone was coming over to see us, and I was ok with that.

Everyone had a memory of Josh and I wanted to hear it. I wanted to hear him kept alive in other's hearts and minds. Because that was where he would live on in this world. Tears came and went, laughter faded and soon we were packing up. The day was over, and my heart was tired.

We loaded up our car and Terry's car with the displays, some of the leftover food and the flower arrangements that had been sent there. We were headed back home, to relax. Liz went back to Terry's and Jeremy and I went in the house, with all the things left from the day. The photos sat in a bag, I didn't hurry to put them back. The displays went in the middle room, which was Josh's toy room, behind the train table. Safe from cat claws. The food made it into the fridge and then we went upstairs to the computer room. Where I had the chance to escape. We got on our game and thanked our friends that were on. The group of friends we had made pooled together and sent one of the flower arrangements to the memorial. It was warming to know that they cared.

Sunday came, and with it rain. Lots of rain, but Liz and I were two determined sisters. I called her and made plans to pick her up around 10am. We were going to the National Civil War Museum today, and I was excited! I was excited because it meant doing something that wasn't going to cause me to cry. I was ready to laugh, and laugh we did. Liz and I don't always get along, but when the moment of need comes we are right there for each other. Ready to bring laughter, an ear or a shoulder, whichever is needed. Today, it was laughter. We talked about anything we could think of on the way there, in which I almost got lost.

"I can't believe I am having such a hard time with this, I've been there before" I joked with her, staring down my phone for it's bad GPS directions.

We finally made it there and parked, just in time too. As we got in and paid our way, a group came out in civil war era attire and began dancing. It was awesome to see the period dance, to period style music and everything. We stood on the steps that took you up to the museum and watched. The girls would twirl and you could see their skirts fluff out and see the joy on their faces. They were doing something they loved.

We walked our way through the different exhibits. Each one brought a different perspective to the time period and some even

Cynthia Complese

made you feel like you were there watching on. They had incredibly life like models and scenes that had timed audio, so you could hear a slave auction taking place and hear people in cells scream out. So many things.

After many hours at the museum Liz and I headed out. I could see the joy on her face from doing something she loved. I was happy to do something that wasn't going to bring me to tears and I was thankful for time invested with her. I knew we had our share of fights, arguments and spats, but above all things she was my sister and I loved her.

The night settled softly in my house. I had dropped Liz off at Terry and Jerry's again and went home. It was hard at home, more so when I was alone. I set my bag at the door and went upstairs. Jeremy was in the computer room and I gave him a kiss on his furry cheek and smiled. I hadn't smiled a real smile in a while. I had just had a good day, after so many sad days. The sad days weren't over though. Tomorrow was Josh's burial. I wasn't ready to think about that. I sat down at my computer and glanced at the small bag on my desk. In it were the cards people had given us and the guest book. I slowly opened the guest book and began to read some of the names in it. I closed the blue leather book and turned my eyes to the Ziploc from the memory table. I slowly opened it and began to read the memories that people had left.

The one that caught my heart the most *"I remember one day at the playground. My boys brought bikes. Josh wanted nothing to do with Christopher's little trike, it was Nick's big two-wheeler that interested him. He was a little boy with BIG ideas."* I thought back to that day. Pushing Josh on the two-wheeler, it had training wheels, but he was determined to ride it. That was his last summer with us. We had bought him a two-wheeler bike the following Christmas and made plans to teach him to ride it, he was happy just sitting on it. I had bought a small bell to put on it for him to ring, he used to chime that and then giggle.

I grabbed for a tissue from my desk. I was crying now, but good cries. The memories were not forgotten and it did not take much to reach back in time and pull them up. I was happy about that. That the memories would flow so easily, I worried that a time would come when they would not.

"I'm heading to bed" Jeremy had said to me, I looked at the clock, it was 1am. It was time for sleep. I shutdown my computer and put away the notes. I changed and climbed into bed next Jeremy, I snuggled up close to him and closed my eyes. I was ready for sleep, good sleep.

Wondrous Love

I woke the next day, knowing what was in store. It was Monday, we were going to bury Josh's body today. I don't know if I was ready or not, but today was it. We had invited a small select group to be with us this day. Nothing huge, just an intimate ceremony. Jeremy and I were going, as was my sister. Terry said she wasn't ready for the pain of it, but Jerry was going to be there. We sent out invites to Ben and Chris as well. Chris was going to be able to make it, but Ben could not get off work.

It was going to be later in the afternoon, around 2pm, so I laid in bed. I pet my cats and enjoyed playing with Nel, Jeremy's cat. The kitten of the house, she loved chasing the light from a flashlight and I was willing to entertain the idea. Her and I played for a little while, when Jeremy rolled over chuckling. "What are you doing?"

I giggled back "Playing with Nel."

He smiled at me and nudged for me to lay back. We snuggled up and rested. It was almost eleven when we got out of bed. It would have been later but the doorbell rang and I needed to get up and answer the door. I would not say it was unimportant, it was a delivery from a local florist. They were delivering a lily, care of my grandparents in Nevada. I smiled and called them to say thank you. I then called Liz, like I had the previous days and planned out when to come pick her up. We got dressed and grabbed McDonald's for lunch. It was too late for breakfast. We ate at Jeremy's parents' house and then loaded up and went to the grocery store. I wanted blue flowers to lay on the site.

We pulled into Rolling Green Cemetery, it was windy and chilly and had snowed briefly that morning. I thought the snow was a gift from Josh, letting us know he loved us. We waited in the car for the hearse to arrive and with it, the casket. I had not brought a coat, I was expecting warmer weather I suppose. The bishop was kind enough to lend me his as we waited for the people from the funeral home to arrive. Chris arrived shortly after we had, the bishop was already there. Jerry arrived right behind Chris, on his motorcycle. We waited. The representative from Rolling Green came down and soon the hearse was pulling into the cemetery. You could see the main entrance from the site. In fact, you could see a statue of Jesus praying behind where Josh was to be buried. Across the way were 4 statues of disciples, that surrounded a raised area of grave sites. The area was beautiful.

They pulled up next to the site and asked about pallbearers. I looked to Jeremy, I had not thought about it. The Bishop volun-

Cynthia Complese

teered right away, as did Jeremy. "Do you think your dad and Chris would be willing?" I asked Jeremy. He nodded back to me and went over to speak with them. Chris had his brand-new baby boy in the car with mama, and was standing right outside the driver door of his car. Jerry was nearby with him, talking about something I am sure. Jeremy went over and spoke with them briefly and soon all three were headed this way. The back of the hearse was opened and I could see the end of the casket. It was white, covered with what looked like brushed velvet. The handles that were on it did not move nor work, they were only decoration. I watched as Jeremy and his Dad, followed by the bishop and Chris, carried Josh's casket to the area they had setup for it. It was small, too small for the set of bars on which they casket was laid. The casket was small in comparison to the area that was set aside for it.

    I sat down in front, near the head of the casket. The bishop began to speak, but I was not hearing his words. My right hand was on Jeremy's knee and my left hand held a bouquet of flowers. Liz was seated to my left and Jeremy's dad to his right. I could hear the bishop's voice, but his words did not resound in my head. I stared at the casket, almost losing focus on reality. As I sat there, I could see Josh, as if through the casket. His body lying there, lifeless and still. Arms folded gently, eyes closed to look as if sleeping. I did not know the outfit Terry had picked out for Josh. It was the one thing I did not want to do, so I had asked her. I could see him in blue, as I always call it a "Josh Blue". It's that royal blue or true blue. I could see peace over his body. I focused back to reality as the bishop began to pray and bring everything to a close.

    I kissed my hand and delicately touched the coffin. I laid the flowers on the top. "I love you buddy" I whispered as my hand came back to my side. I slid off the bishop's coat and handed it to him. "Thank you" I spoke, between breaths and tears. Reality was sinking in. Our son was gone from this earth.

    Jeremy had bowling that night, and I was ready for a night of something closer to normal. While I love my sister dearly, us together all the time and we grate on each other. I did extend the invitation for her to come with us, but she expressed that it really was not her scene.

"I think I am ok without the drinking and such. Besides, it doesn't bother me spending a night in." She explained to us as we dropped her off that evening.

"Are you sure?" I said, while secretly I was ready for a night of regular, I didn't want to hurt my sister's feelings either.

"I'm sure." she confirmed.

"Ok, we'll see you tomorrow then." I gave her a hug and Jeremy and I headed home to relax and change before heading out.

Cynthia Complese

3
Faith Propels Us

We arrived at the bowling center a little after 5pm. It wasn't going to start until 7, but we thought about grabbing a bite while we were there. We arrived in the door and Eric (his team captain) was already in the bar with several other buddies. I wasn't sure what the night was going to look like, but it was going to be a wild one. I couldn't tell you what Jeremy scored or how he bowled. I think tonight was more about him, and him coping. He was drunk, more than drunk. I had never seen him this way. The entire bowling league knew what about Josh. In fact it was pretty often that Josh would come in with me and say hi to everyone. They had donated some money from a 50/50 they run towards Josh and everyone was buying Jeremy drinks that night. The bartender was generous with the shots and the Alabama Slammers kept coming. Several shots and 3 drinks later, Jeremy was cut off, but it was too late. He was drunk.

The guys helped me gather up his gear, and helped me get him to the car. I remember I had pulled the car up to the front door and they helped him in. I was very thankful that I was driving. My only concern was getting pulled over and them smelling the alcohol on his breath, because it filled the car.

I continued to laugh along with it, I wasn't mad. I knew how he felt. I called Chris, I knew he would get a good laugh. I put Chris on speaker and Jeremy started rambling words off to him. I was rolling and so was Jeremy. I drove through Burger King on the way home, I was hungry, all the while Jeremy and Chris had a drunk conversation. I was laughing hard and by the time we got home, Chris was on the other end rolling. We got off the phone with Chris and I helped Jeremy in the house. His words were slurred and he was stumbling. I helped him up the back step and in the house. He sat in the dining room, repeatedly telling me how I was pretty. I would chuckle and smile at him and then helped him take his shoes off. I helped him up the steps "Don't you make me fall" I had laughed at him. I didn't know what he needed or how to help. If that meant holding him to get him to bed right now, I was willing.

Cynthia Complese

He fell into bed, fully dressed and that was it. He was snoring before I could get his shirt off. It was the next morning that struck me. When we woke up he shared something with me that tugged at my spirit. Jeremy began to share the dream he had, after his night of drunken rivalry.

"It was Josh, we were in a room, like the one from the Ronald McDonald House, but not quite. I said 'hey buddy!' and walked over to him and hugged him. I glanced over to the lights and end tables, where there was an outlet. Josh was suddenly as tall as me and grabbed my head in his hands, looked me in the eyes and said 'Dad, don't you dare look at that outlet'."

I could feel my eyes widen as he recounted this to me. I had never experienced what we were experiencing, but I felt comfort in knowing that God's hand was in this. We drove Liz to the airport that day and said our goodbyes. It was a long journey to this point, from where we were when we picked her up to where we were now. We watched her pass the TSA area and then headed back to the car and back to our home. The time had come to find some new form of normal.

Morning came slow and I when I awoke I could hear birds outside. It took some time to realize what time it was and what season we were in. It wasn't spring yet, but it was warming up. I rolled over and snuggled up to Jeremy. Our plan that day was simple, to do nothing. I just wanted to be with Jeremy, however I knew I needed to do laundry and I knew we needed some groceries.

Jeremy went with me to get groceries and helped me bring them in the house. We were inseparable during this time. He was all I wanted next to me, his presence brought comfort. He always had a way of making me laugh in the toughest of times and I could enjoy the moment. We get all the groceries in the house and we were laughing about something one of the cats had done. When his phone goes off. It's a text from his friend Chris. They were on the way to the hospital with his son, Braden.

We told Chris to keep us posted and we would be out there soon. I felt at peace going out there to support them. Jeremy and I finished putting away groceries and we took the drive to Hershey. We pulled in the parking lot and made the long walk to the front door, we walked our way back to the ER where Chris and his family were. The look in his eyes when he saw us was remarkable. I gave him a hug and I can't recall a time Chris hugged me as tight as he did then. Chris and I never really got

Wondrous Love

along, but it was in these days that he and I connected and I saw him as family.

Our wait there was a slow one. Tests were being done and results were waited on. We laughed and joked, like our group was good at. We never were the serious types, there was a joke and laugh for everything. Even in the toughest of times we would smile. My phone rang and I stepped aside to answer it. It was Courtney. We were confirming our day together tomorrow. I said I was at the hospital, but that I think I needed it. So, no matter what, we were still on.

They moved Braden up to the PIMCU when they found that he had a hematoma in his brain. It was a blessing that they caught this, and we were praying they caught it early enough. We took turns being in the family room and being back with Chris and his family. The nursing staff recognized me and the grief counselor asked me why we were there. I explained to him about Braden and what was going on. He looked at me with an astonishing smile and said if we needed anything to ask. I smiled back and headed back to the family room, where Jeremy was sitting with Ben and the others. I had only gone back to ask Braden's mom a question, I was headed back out to be with them.

When I came back to the family room Chris, Jeremy and Ben were playing one of the games in the closet. I am not even sure what the game was, but they were laughing pretty hard. I went over and made myself a cup of coffee and sat down with them. When the game was over, Chris turned to Jeremy and I and spoke words I will never forget.

"Thank you for coming out, but I can't believe you guys are here."

"Where else would we be?" I responded to him, with a small smile. Jeremy standing next to me nodded in agreement. Where else would we be? Sitting at home was not any better than sitting here, at least here we could be of use in distractions. It was early in the morning at this point, around 4am. Jeremy and I said our goodbyes and headed home. We said we would be back later that afternoon and we would bring food. So, we drove home. I told Jeremy I was headed to Courtney's for a day of relaxing and for him to get a nap and I would be home soon.

It was a little after 9am when I got to Courtney's home. We laughed and talked, sharing stories and we talked about a book she gave me to read. It was quickly approaching noon and I needed to wake Jeremy and get us back to Hershey. I had promised Chris we would bring lunch. I rushed out of her place and went home. I roused Jeremy from his sleep and we headed to Hospital.

We were not at the hospital long when I felt this draw to leave. I looked at Jeremy with sadness, I didn't want to leave them, but I felt I needed to not be in the hospital.

"I am sure they will understand." he assured me. I gave half a smile and we said our goodbyes. I hugged Chris and realized, Jeremy was right. Everyone understood.

It was the night of March 10, 2011. I had just returned to my friend Courtney's home. I was there earlier that morning and had to rush out the door. I was thankful to return to her home. The comfort in her home is remarkable and the feeling of the Lord is so strong there and has become stronger since this day.

I had just left the hospital with my husband. Chris's 7-day old son was in the Milton Hershey Medical Center, in the PIMCU. We had spent the previous night there, supporting him. When we went back there the afternoon of the 10th, I felt as though I was not supposed to be there. Something was drawing me away. We left at 6pm and headed home. The drive home I continued to tell my husband about visiting at Courtney's home and how I had felt at her home. How I was having the urge to go back there.

"Before I left Courtney's, I asked her about reading 'My Time in Heaven'." I began to recall the moments with my husband.

I had asked her "When you read do you see what he is talking about like you are standing there with him?"

She told me "No. Do you?"

I said "Yes."

"Praise Jesus!" came from her lips. As she spoke those words I saw a flash in her living room window of a figure. I didn't know at the time what it was, then I saw a gold flash in her sliding glass door, to my left. I turned to look and it was gone.

"I have to go, we'll talk more, later." I said as I literally ran out the door.

As I told my husband about this moment I felt drawn back even stronger. Like I had to go back to Courtney's. When we got home I asked my husband about his spiritual beliefs and how he felt about all of this. He told me he believed in God and Jesus and that was as far as it went. I looked at him and said "I need to

Wondrous Love

go back to Courtney's. You get in your nap and I will see you when I get home."

I immediately called Courtney and went to her home. It was 8:00 in the evening when I arrived. Upon arriving we began to listen to Richard Sigmund on Sid Roth, he is the author of "My Time in Heaven". After that we watched about 2 minutes of "23 minutes in Hell" with Bill Wiese, after that we tried to load and watch Choo Thomas, as she spoke about "Heaven is so Real". That was buffering and taking a while, so we went to Brandon Hess and listened to his testimony of him coming into his gifts of being able to see into the spiritual realm.

"Since hearing that I can now share with you what I saw today in your home," I began to tell Courtney.

"What did you see!?" she exclaimed at me.

I told her about the figure I saw in her window. "Who was it?" was the response Courtney had given me.

"I don't know."

"It was an Angel!!" she was so excited. "Praise you Jesus!" I began to giggle, while I was a little confused, she was very excited.

"This is a gift," she continued "from the Holy Spirit." She placed her right hand on my left shoulder, thanking the Lord and Jesus for the gifts I had received, for the ability of me being able to see into the spiritual realm.

When she did that I felt a cool and calming wave come over me. I gasped as I felt calming fingertips, just above the base of my shoulder blades. They were pressing into me, just enough to let me know. I felt as though if they had placed their full hand against my back I would have been overcome with calm and peace. "I feel, what seems to be fingertips on my back, giving off this cool calm." I began to tell Courtney.

"Praise you Jesus!" came from Courtney's lips. I looked past her and to what was my right, where 3 figures appeared before me. I felt my eyes widen and I thought they were going to pop out of my head.

"The.. there.. there's 3 angels... oh.. oh.. over there." I stuttered, with amazement, as I pointed in their direction.

"What color are they?" she had asked me with so much excitement.

"I don't know", all the while thinking to myself 'They have color?!?'.

"Well look!"

I turned my eyes back to them and began to see color form where an outline once stood. It was almost as if I was being told the color but not exactly. "White... white, blue... 2 white and 1 blue. White, blue, white... white, blue white, like a baby blue. Like a soft-focus picture, an aura around them."

"What's the color of the one behind you?" Courtney asked.

"I don't know!"

"Look!"

"No, I'm not ready. It just feels like glory, immense glory! If that makes any since." I had said. My head was starting to spin and I was starting to feel shaky.

"Ya! The glory of God!" she continued on "This is the kind of stuff Tyler sees."

"I see multiple flashes" I began to feel intimidated and concerned.
Courtney began to pray, "Lord please release Angels of protection and comfort to come down..."

I felt my physical eyes get larger as my spiritual eyes squinted open. "There is an angel, right here." I pointed to my left, which happened to be the back of the couch and an exterior wall to her home. "I can't tell if it is outside, like I am seeing through the wall or not. When Tyler sees, the Angels come down does he say he sees them fly in a circle or just come down?"

"Tyler said to me, about the big blue angel, 'Fly circle 'round mommy house, fly sky home.' He also said when he saw them

Wondrous Love

outside of our van, that he saw angels flying in circles." Courtney explained quickly, but excitedly.

"Ya!" my eyes got HUGE. "They are flying in a circle, so fast! I can't really make them out, they are just blurring."

Courtney read Psalm 91:1-16. I asked her to go back to about the angels guarding. When she went back to verse 11, *"For he will command his Angels concerning you. To guard you in all your ways."* "Ya! When you said that the Angels stood at attention, like 'Yes, we will guard you!'" I exclaimed.

"Jesus is ruler of all of heaven and earth," Courtney began, "all of creation bows to the name of Jesus."

As she said that I saw a sea of animals, every animal I could imagine and some I had never seen. They were all bowing down, as I watched them. They were all intermingled with each other. Lions stood beside giraffes, zebras and gophers were side by side. All "modge podged" together. I was looking above and to the side of them, when it felt as though I was a camera panning down to be beside them. They were all on clouds and the sea of animals seemed to disappear off in the horizon. When I came beside them they were kneeling in the direction of Courtney's kitchen, where there were these bright beams of golden rays.

"Who do you see? Look!"

"No!" I told her, the feeling of glory coming from that direction was immense.

"That's Jesus! Where two or more are gathered, he is there. So, he is here, whether we see him or not." Courtney told me.

"There is music playing, I can't hear it, but I know it's playing." I gasped! "I just saw Josh! His eyes were huge and he was cheering. His hands were clapping faster than they ever could here on earth. He was clapping SO hard! It was a flash, but it felt like I saw 3 minutes of time."

"He's cheering because he is watching his mother come to know Jesus Christ as her Lord and Savior. This gift you've been given, because you told the Lord you would praise him no matter what. It's kind of like the prayer covenant I made with the Lord, when I asked for Tyler to be healed. That if he would heal his heart, everyone would know that it was God who healed him. I know that the only reason that Tyler is here, is because of that prayer."

"I see someone nodding their head, yes, to what you are saying" I told Courtney.

"I know Tyler will receive a brand-new heart from God."

"It's a Blue Angel nodding their head 'yes' to what you are saying." I described
"Ok, Lord, I am going to go the whole way. I am going to ask that you release an Angel to the warehouse to get the heart that has been promised to Tyler and bring it and put it in his body."
I gasped and smiled and saw an Angel smiling.

"Ok Lord, I know you also have timing and that this may not be the time yet." Courtney continued. I let her know that the angel I saw was nodding their head 'yes' now.

"An orange angel just came in behind you, and I was shown this tall angel. It reminds me of the Angel Moroni that sits atop the LDS Temples, with the long trumpet and everything." I excitedly exclaimed.

"Everyone wants to know why we are here." Courtney began to teach. "We are God's children, why do you have children? To love them! He wants to love and pour blessings out on us. That's why us fellowshipping like this, this is what we are supposed to do. Save souls, each soul is God's child and he wants them to be with him."

I gasped! "There are 6 to 12, yes 12, children sitting on the floor beside us... the girls are in white dresses the boys are in white shirts and pants. They had different hair colors, black, brown, blond, all of it. They are between the ages of 2 and 5, sitting cross legged on the floor."

Courtney took her turn in gasping and stated "Yes! This is just like in that book "6 Big Big Big Angels", about Victoria! These are children who were terminated, miscarried, killed or died young and they are coming to hear us talk about the Lord and to learn. Do not fear hell. God did not create that for us. It was created for Satan and his fallen angels."

Wondrous Love

"Just as you said that, 2 more boys arrived. A 10-year-old and a 16-year-old. They are sitting on your love seat." I told her. The 10-year-old was sitting to the right of the 16-year-old, but I did not mention that at that time. "There is a little boy, standing near the love seat." (He was standing near the corner of the love seat by the 10-year-old boy, but I did explain it at that time.)

"Is there anything special about him?" Courtney had asked.

"I don't know, I can't really tell."

"Lord," Courtney began to pray, "if there is anything we are to know about this boy please let it be revealed to us."

As she prayed things began to become clearer. "He appears to be about the size of Josh and Tyler." I told her.

"There are no booboo's in heaven." Courtney continued.

"All the children cheered at that." I told her. My physical eyes became HUGE as I saw an Angel come in. "There is an Angel standing behind the boy by the loveseat. He... wow!" I gasped.

"He's huge! Like your ceiling is extending to fit him in. I've never seen a warrior angel, but yes! I am being told he is a warrior and that he is a HE!!" My eyes shifted to Courtney, I did not know what was happening but my body began to shake, like my body was resonating to come into tune with my spirit.

"Lord, if there is anything you want to reveal about this little boy, please reveal it to Cynthia and me. If there is anything we are supposed to know about this little boy with the Angel, that you just reveal it now." Courtney prayed.

At that very instant I watched as the Angel picked up the little boy, although I am not sure how, and came towards me head first. His face seemed to be inches from mine and I was overwhelmed with this feeling of "We love you!" and he flew past my face and was gone. I began to explain this event to Courtney.

"The warrior angel was intimidating, amazing! He had dark brown hair, a little lighter than yours" I began to explain to Courtney, "it was straight at the top but the ends became curly. The eyes were bright blue and piercing. His face was full of power."

Cynthia Complese

"You know who that was right?" Courtney stated. We both began to tear up. "That was Josh." We began to cry.

As the time went on, we had to stop. There seemed to be a beacon over the house for the Angels to know that we were talking about the Lord. It was like they all thought that we were having a party and this where they wanted to be. Brandon Hess describes coming into the gift as putting on 3D glasses. Which is very true. Everything looks so different, like you are seeing some things for the first time, although you have looked at them a thousand times before.

I left her home, afraid at first to walk into the dark. I knew the things I had heard to be true now. I had seen parts of hell and parts of heaven. I knew the enemy lived in the dark I did not want to be in it. Courtney prayed over me and I knew I needed to conquer the fear and head home.

While driving home, I saw angels surrounding the car, I had no sleep in the past 48 hours now, and was exhausted. I made it home safely, the events of the night spinning through my head. I did not know how to explain what just happened. I went in the door of my home and made it upstairs. I left the hall light on that night, I did not want to be in the dark. I curled up close to Jeremy and we slept.

I woke the next morning, Jeremy still sleeping, this was his last week off. I was headed to meet Courtney early. I just had to talk to her again. My head was still spinning from the night before and I could not describe how I felt, only thing I knew is that I needed a bible.

I drove down main street in New Cumberland. As I stopped to allow a pedestrian cross, I felt the Lord's love for that person. All I could feel was how much God loved them. Everything was new, new feelings, new looks everything. I pulled onto Courtney's lot and turned the car off. I knocked lightly and she opened the door. I smiled at Evangeline as she came running in the room, and fast behind her was Tyler, my son's best friend. Tyler hid behind his mom, which wasn't normal for him, giggling.

"Hi Evie. Hi Tyler." I spoke to them. Evie gave a soft "hi" and Tyler stuck his head out from behind his mom and giggled. He whispered something to his mom and then they had both ran off to play again. I chuckled and sat down at the kitchen table.

"He said he saw angels." Courtney told me with a smile. I didn't know what my life was turning into, but what I thought to

Wondrous Love

be normal was off by a lot. We spoke a little and I told Courtney I needed a bible. She agreed to follow me to a Christian book store where I could try to find a bible. It was a ten-minute drive from her place to the store, but worth the drive. I got there and got out of the car, Courtney helped the kids out of the car. She shared with me that every time they were not able to see my car that Tyler would exclaim "I can't see Him!". We spoke further on that and believed he was talking about Jesus.

I started to sort through bible after bible, I could not find one that spoke to me. So, I settled for a simple NIV Bible. By this time, Courtney had headed out with the kids, they were restless and ready for snacks and quiet time. I understood. I paid for my book and a cover for it and headed home. I was excited to own it, but didn't know where to start. The book seemed intimidating to me and I didn't know if I was ready for this.

I got home and Jeremy and I headed out to eat. We didn't eat at home during this time. It was hard to get used to the idea of only cooking for two. Jeremy and I began talking about our upcoming vacation. It was odd to us, how we had planned this vacation without even really knowing how badly we were going to need it. Both of us were quickly looking forward to April, our third wedding anniversary, but also our first vacation together. It was meant to be a time for us to rekindle our marriage, we needed that time together now more than ever.

I still needed to figure out how to tell Jeremy about all that I had been through. It was my experience, but Jeremy and I had not had any kind of "spiritual" talks. Jesus never came up, God never came up, this was just not stuff that we talked about. Jeremy was about to start going back to work, and we were about to see what the new "normal" looked like for us. I didn't know what I was doing with what I saw now. Even as we would go out to eat I would see, but I didn't know how to tell Jeremy what I was seeing. This was all very new to me as well.

Cynthia Complese

4
Learning to Heal

I began spending my afternoons at Panera Bread, laptop, and bible in tow, I would sit there all day long. Browse the web, read the bible, and hide away from the empty home. With Jeremy back at work, I wasn't sure how I was going to cope through the days ahead. I was still not working, but I wasn't ready to work either. I was broken and in need of repair.

Somehow, I knew that I was already beginning to be repaired and made new, I just wasn't sure how. I could still feel and see angelic beings around me as I would sit and work on this book in the cafe. I wasn't sure what was really going on or why I had been given this amazing gift. I wasn't even sure how I was going to adjust to having it or if I ever would.

Jeremy and I had finally talked about what I had encountered at Courtney's and the things I would see. It was all very new to me and most of the time I would ask him questions, and try to make something out of what I was seeing or why. Jeremy had attended catholic schools, so he had a better understanding of the bible then I did. So, I would turn to him with my questions and often times we would turn to the internet. It was nice to be able to share with him what I saw. Things were still a little awkward, I wasn't completely comfortable with seeing yet.

Jeremy and I began to prepare our home for a visitor. A friend of mine was going on vacation for a short time and needed a sitter, for her dog. So, we made sure that things of importance were picked up and that he couldn't "accidentally" get in trouble. We cleared a space in the dining room for his crate and a spot for his bowls. We thought we were ready... sort of. I knew it would be nice to have company in the house that wasn't the cats, but I also knew the cats were going to be very mad at me.

March 27th came with a swift arrival, and Buddy came bounding to our door. His tail wagged like crazy and I surely thought he would have fallen over with that much momentum. He came in and ran around sniffing everything and chasing the cats. (Which they quickly learned to stay upstairs away from Buddy.) We spoke with them briefly as they brought in his crate and food.

Cynthia Complese

Wanting to make sure we had all the details right before they left for their vacation. I also wanted to reassure them that Buddy was safe.

The nights we uneventful as Buddy was with us. I would walk him in the morning and Jeremy would walk with us in the evening. I started to remember how much fun I had teaching tricks and training dogs. I was sort of sad when the day came and Buddy was headed home. Jeremy and I began discussing the idea of getting a dog, and if so what kind. I had never put much thought into it, until Buddy came to stay. We knew we wanted a dog after he left, just not that breed. We needed to find the breed that was right for us.

Jeremy spent the next few days researching online what breed would be good for us, the final decision came. We were getting an English Mastiff. I was so excited, but dubious. I started to question if we were meant to do this or if this was us doing what we wanted. I was ready to send out the deposit to the breeder and we would pick up the dog when we got back from vacation. The check in hand, I didn't have the address to the breeder to mail the check.

As I began to feel doubt overwhelm me I started to pray. By this point, I knew doubt was not of God and if he wanted us to do this, then the doubt would go and I would be at peace again. Sure enough, the doubt left and I was back at peace and just in time for my phone to vibrate and let me know that I had a new email. It was the mailing address to send the deposit in. We were officially getting a dog.

But let him ask in faith, with no doubting, for the one who doubts is like a wave of the sea that is driven and tossed by the wind.
- James 1:6

It was 3am on April 14th, I was lying in bed, wide awake. I was thinking about how much Josh would have loved to be here when we brought the puppy home. I started to hear his voice saying "puppity!" I smiled lightly as my eyes closed. My mind still on little Joshua.

It was not a surprise that my mind went to him right now. I was recovering from teeth extractions, the pain waking me often in the middle of the night. But also, the remembrance of when I came to from being under for the extractions. I was in the recovery room and the only thing I could tell my husband was "I saw Josh". I remember I cried as the words left and even when he told me not to speak, I had to. I had to tell him, if for no other reason than that I would remember.

Wondrous Love

As my eyes closed I began to see a white fog surround me, as it lifted I was in this clearing I was beginning to know so well. Then, suddenly, as if I had blinked, I was sitting at a picnic table, in a park. It was brilliantly lit and wonderfully light, like the sun hadn't shown for days and was finally out again. Josh and I were sitting next to each other putting together a puzzle, like we were picking up where we left off (though I don't remember being there before). We weren't even trying to figure out what piece needed to go where. We already knew, we were just putting them in their place.

"Dad and I are getting a dog" I told him.

"That's wonderful!" he exclaimed to me, his beautiful brown eyes smiling at me then he returned quickly back to the puzzle.

"What do you think we should name her?" I had asked. Josh continued to pick up puzzle pieces and lay them down where they belonged.

"Josh, what should we name her?" I asked again after a period of silence. He looked at me quizzically. "You're still a member of the family, Josh. So you get the chance to help name her."

I saw a smile come across his face as he happily exclaimed, "Daisy!"

I smiled back at him and then I was awake, in a dark room with Josh's cat on my chest. After speaking with my husband, we both agreed, even though we have not met our dog yet, Daisy would be a good name.

I was ready to come home and get our new dog. We had been gone for 3 nights on vacation and I could not wait! We drove the 3 hours' home and dropped off our things, said hello to our cats and quickly buzzed off to get our new addition. I couldn't remember being so happy in so long. It felt good to know joy again. We arrived on the lot where the breeder lived. Daisy's mom was "guarding" bones they just put out for the dogs and the breeder brought out the 2 little girls he had left. A little apricot colored pup came out first, and I chuckled at how she tripped over her own feet. But she was very stubborn and slightly smaller than the other puppy they brought out. We knew that was our Daisy the moment we saw her!

Cynthia Complese

She was fawn colored with a beautiful black mask, I picked her up in my arms and she nuzzled right into my neck, and I knew she was ours. Jeremy wrote the check as I just hugged her close. I could feel my heart begin to mend with every sniff she gave to my face. She was my girl, my baby! We rode to the pet store next, to get the things she would need for the house. A crate, some bowls and food, not to mention all the toys and collars and leashes. Oh ya, she was about to be spoiled!

Jeremy's mom met us at the store to help us haul home the crate. We already knew it wasn't going to fit in our car. I was excited! We enrolled her in a puppy class that same day, as well. With our favorite trainer, Dawn! We'd known her for years and we were excited to introduce her to Daisy, but I was nervous about telling her about Josh.

As we were driving home I started to recall how I felt when we first came home from the hospital, without Josh. I felt that I needed to tell everyone, because then they couldn't catch me off guard by asking me. We even thought about telling the crossing guard that sat outside our home.

We got our little Daisy home and the house seemed, brighter. We were laughing again, and oh how she made us laugh (and still does). We never thought that such a little thing could brighten our lives so much after what we'd gone through.

Right here I could say that Daisy was all I needed and I felt healed, but it wouldn't be truth. I still cried and wept, I still hurt. Although I had reason to laugh now, I was still in pain. I had begun to grow in the Lord, in a way I could not put to words, except that I was on fire. I prayed the fire would never dim and I would always have this passion for God and to do His will and share His word. My husband helped me build a website for a blog, so I could start making posts about what I was learning and opening an environment to share in. While no one ever went there, I was able to learn amazing things there.

During my time of transition and phasing, I was learning increasingly more about God. Who He was, what He was capable of. So much that I could not, even now, begin to put it into words. I was learning that I was healed by the stripes of Jesus. So, being that I had been diagnosed with Bipolar, I was done with it. I didn't want to be on medications and I didn't want to suffer this any longer. So I would cry out to God every night, that i wanted to be healed from it. The healing would last for a day or 2 and then it would be back. While at a friend's house for bible study one night, I brought up that i wanted to be healed from this. So we began to pray over me. One gentleman was well versed in

Wondrous Love

scripture and was teaching what he had learned to us, began to call out demons and roots to die in the light.

I will be honest, I can't recall the exact words he said, but I recall how I felt. I remember as he began to pray, I could not move my mouth. I could not agree or praise or move. I was frozen in place. I felt like a jagged dagger dig into my calves as he continued to pray. I remember wanting to scream and I couldn't. I remember wanting to cry and I could not get my eyes to release a tear. Soon the pain was gone and my legs buckled and fell back onto the chair that was behind me. I felt a million times lighter. As though the burden of what I was carrying had lifted and was gone.

I knew, in that moment, I was healed. I went home that night and dumped all my pills down the drain and in the trash. I was no longer going to be a slave to this disease, Jesus had healed me! For the first time in a very long time, my mind was silent. I was sleeping soundly and I felt joy. I was truly happy.

I enrolled in the Kingdom Living School at my church, that summer. I was watching online, because of the nearly 1 hour drive to get there. I was learning so much from an amazing teacher, Dan Mohler. The identity he showed me was completely different then the identity I had been taught.

One day, I remember listening to him to speak and he talked about a vision. In this vision the person saw the hands of Jesus pick up their child. As he went on to talk he said that most would say the child is gone, but in his perspective, he was saying that the child was in the hands of the great physician. They were about to be healed! My jaw dropped open and I was amazed. In that moment, God was talking directly to me. I recall little else from that day, only that God was showing me a perspective shift. That my perspective created my reality, and if I wanted things to be different i needed to shift how I saw things.

In this instance, I had the same vision. I watched the hands of Jesus lift up my Joshua. But if my perspective was different, then everything could be different. I began to learn that faith was a muscle and that if I didn't exercise it, it would grow weak.

I began to exercise my faith as I would paint. I needed to learn how to do things and I had to have faith in God that He would show me.

The steps of a good man are ordered by the Lord,
And He delights in his way.
- Psalm 37:23

Cynthia Complese

    I was learning to lean not on my own understanding. I was learning to trust in scripture and speak it out. I was learning to pray according to His word. I wish I could say that healing came in an instant, but it did not. Comfort came quickly, peace came quickly, but healing took time. Holidays were tough. As the first Christmas without Josh quickly approached, I wasn't sure how to handle this. I was about to start a new job and everything was shifting. The kingdom school was over and I was trying to hold tight to everything I had learned.

    Summer was over now, Daisy was growing, I was growing in God and thought that I was ready to return to work. I went looking for a photography job, that was my passion before, when Josh was with us, so it seemed right. I was hired on by a school photography organization. I was with them for one fall season. It was all I needed though, to realize, I couldn't do photography for another company again. I needed freedom with it, I had ideas and my creativity was not allowed on the clock. They did contests and such, but that didn't really matter much to me. I wasn't a contest type person. I wanted my photography to make a difference.

    I would go to the store and realize how badly I wanted to speak to the mom who just slapped her child's hand and told them no so harshly while they waited at the checkout. Or the dad that all but tossed his child to their mother because they were throwing a fit. The parents that took for granted the love of their children, I wanted to find a way to reach them. I didn't know how to, but I knew I wanted to.

    I was getting ready for work at the photography company one afternoon, when a friend of mine contacted me, it was October, I wasn't expecting the news that I was receiving. Another friend of ours, her nephew had gone to be with Jesus, he was only a few months old. While there were complications, I wasn't expecting this news. I had been praying for him to pull through. I cried heavily. I left work and came home, crying still. I didn't know how to cope with this fresh pain. Suddenly, my fingers had a hunger to paint. I'd sketched here and there, mostly of things that I was seeing while people spoke. I had never actually painted... until now. I ran quickly to the craft store and bought a canvas and a few brushes and then came home. I had some leftover basic colors in acrylics from classes I had taken. With those and my new brushes I began to paint my first canvas. To say it was an amazing masterpiece would not be truth, but it was beautiful. I felt release as I watched the painting take place and I realized, I wasn't just painting. God was showing me how to paint. I would look at the paint and He would highlight the one I

Wondrous Love

needed to use, and He would highlight the brush to use. He would show me before the paint and brush even met what I needed to do.

My eyes lit up as I started to notice, that God was healing my heart while He taught me to paint. I felt elated! I smiled so big, the biggest in months. I had no idea it was possible. When it was done, the painting was of a sun, you couldn't tell exactly if it was rising or setting, it all but filled the canvas. There was a green bit of land in front of it and a purple sky behind it. Light beamed off the sun and in the green land I wrote the last half of Psalm 30:5 *Weeping may endure for the night, but joy comes in the morning.*

My cursive was not pretty, I was not good at any form of script. So, I wrote it very carefully in print with India ink and then I wrapped it in paper to deliver that weekend at the service. I had taken a picture of it prior to wrapping it up, because I never wanted to forget the first painting I had ever done. I didn't sign it, but I included a letter with it. I was excited to give it away.

It wasn't long after that I was approached about painting at my church. It was during the worship part of service, how I felt my fingers flow and my hands would hunger to worship the Lord in such an amazing way. And I would look forward to the end of the service, when I would ask God, to whom would this painting go to, and I would wait and scan the crowd. The He would highlight someone. I would get so excited, because I knew He had something awesome for them. To say my favorite part was giving it away would be so true. While I enjoyed painting, I loved the look on someone's face when they received it even more.

It wasn't always that way though, I recall the first time I painted on the stage. I was nervous and my hands were shaking so bad I dropped my brush. I was on the verge of tears and called out to God. "Daddy, I can't do this."

"What's wrong, child?" He responded to me so softly, I will never forget.

"They're watching me..."

"No, it's just you and me up here, and they are watching Me. Come on, let's paint." I could feel Him smiling over me as I was filled with such peace. Whenever the Lord calls me to paint, I feel His peace wash over me as I take my spot for worship, and I know that I am doing what He called me to.

It was through painting that the healing took place. From spending time alone with God, painting with my favorite worship

Cynthia Complese

music on in the background. Just painting whatever the Lord started to show me. Sometimes my hands would hunger to paint so bad, that I would end up sketching the image before I would even have the chance to paint it. It took time for me to realize that I needed to face situations with courage and know that God would show up and carry me.

It wasn't easy, I thought it would be, but I was wrong. I didn't know what this walk was going to look like, but I knew I was going to do this. I was determined to stay on fire for God and not back slide! I was not going to lose my grip on what God had given me.

There was so much more God wanted me to learn. I had to see what our relationship looked like and find out what I was created for. The more I searched for Him the more I learned about me. The more that God revealed of my past and who I was, and how I got where I was today. During this time, I was a double dipping wild woman. I was attending Saturday night services and Sunday services. I could not get enough worship and prayer. I was so hungry, like I had not eaten in months. I thought I was being fed a feast, but it was only a crumb. I was hungry for more, so I cried out and sought after it. The deepest part of me was crying out for more of Him, the deepest in God responded back!

Deep calls unto deep at the noise of Your waterfalls;
All Your waves and billows have gone over me. - Psalm 42:7

Little did I know of what was to come, only that I wanted more of God. I knew He was faithful to respond to fill my hunger. I just had to continue to walk it out.

5
Walking It Out

My reality was wrong. I was so determined at first to not lose what I had been so lovingly given. But then months later I realized, it had faded... I had faded. I thought I was walking this out like I should have been, I thought I was doing things right. Why was this fading? Why was I not opening my mouth to pray anymore? What was going on? What had happened to me?

I'd gone to work at FedEx after my photography season was over. I was excited to be there. Get paid to work out? Yes please! I didn't expect the walk to be as hard as it was. I underestimated the enemy and I over estimated myself. It didn't happen in a an instant. It was a slow fade. By the time I realized what happened, my joy wasn't gone but I had started to complain. Things would come from my mouth and my eyes would open wide like "Oh my goodness! Did I just say that! Where did that come from?" I would be shocked at things that came from my mouth and I realized, it was easier to walk this out when I was at home feeding on the word and fellowship with God all day. But when I had to decrease the time we spent together to come to work, because I could no longer do chores during that time, it became hard.

It was hard to find fellowship at work. Few wanted to talk about Jesus, but many were respectful of where I was. I couldn't put a name to how I felt, but I knew I wanted to preach His word. Then one of my co-workers asked me, "Are you a pastor?" and almost instinctively I said "Not yet." It was that day that changed something in me. I began to realize how I was acting and wisdom came to me about things that I didn't understand. I don't even know why I responded that way. As I write this I am still not 'yet' a pastor. I do have the hunger to shepherd His sheep though. I knew I had a long way still to go.

I started to determine in myself I wasn't walking up to work without my bible. We weren't allowed to bring our phones up, so I had to settle for my big hunk'in bible. Which is good to me, it's my favorite! It's a New King James Study Bible that was a gift

Cynthia Complese

from a dear friend shortly after I was saved. I love highlighting it in different colors and making notes in it. Feeling the weight of the promise in my hand.

I didn't know how this was going to work out, but I determined in myself that in the 5 months it took for my light to start to fade, I was coming back brighter than before! Let me back up a little. When I talk about fading, I'm talking about the fire that God put in me for Him. It slowed to just embers. I wasn't quick to pray and I wasn't quick rebuke the enemy. I had silenced my tongue, or more so allowed the enemy to. I wasn't quick to walk away from things that offended me and I was quick to join with co-workers to complain. But it wasn't just at work.

At home I had slacked on praying over my husband and our home. I had stopped praying over our animals and even myself. I started to allow my time to become "busy", we have an acronym for it even *"being under satan's yoke"*. Meaning I was allowing the enemy to come in and occupy my time for God with distractions.

My husband and I were always gamers, but my heart was convicted to walk away from it when I was saved, and I did. But as I back slid I walked back to the game. I never removed it from my computer, but I did stop paying for it and I had stopped even being at my computer when I was on fire. Then, I was playing every free chance I had. It became an escape, from stress. Why was I even stressed? Why was I even playing? When I began to realize why I was playing and what was going on I cried. I remember repenting and declaring into the atmosphere that I was going to be hotter for God then ever!

I started to face challenges. I was ready to stop gaming and my husband wasn't. I was ready to chase after God with radical obedience and my husband wasn't. I didn't know what to do or how to handle this. I didn't have anyone modeling this out for me in my life. All I had was prayer and God, I don't think I needed much more though. It's here that I want to share the scripture that keeps me fighting through this;

Now faith is the substance of things hoped for, the evidence of things not seen.
- Hebrews 11:1

I refuse to give up faith in God, that my family's hearts will find Him and that my husband and I will chase radically after God. I won't let the sin around me to produce sin in me, any longer. I was ready to put an end to what the enemy was trying

Wondrous Love

to do in my life. I began to pay closer attention to what was going on around me. The words I would say, things I would do. I started to force myself to pray again. It was hard at first but it flowed so smoothly after a few days. Even know I pray that what happened then was a test, but I am thankful to be fighting back towards where I was... and further.

It's hard to see things correctly until you admit that you might be your own hindrance. I had been praying for things to come, but I started to notice, it was my own fault they weren't here. I wasn't in the place to believe for them like I should. Am I blessed to know this? Yes! I am also thankful to have the courage to admit it. It's not an easy thing to admit, when you're alone in your prayer closet and asking God why things aren't happening, it hits. It's me! I cried so hard, with a weeping I had never had. I felt so bad that I had hindered the move of God in my life. I had put Him in a box and stopped Him from moving. I never wanted that.

God started to show me what He always asked from His children. I was shown a chapel, it was small but beautiful. Inside the chapel were stables, made for horses. I was confused. I looked around and the stables had horses in them, but not your 'standard' horse, these horses resembled a phoenix. In that they were of fire not of flesh. I heard the Spirit of the Lord say to me "I am not a stallion to be stabled", as I stared at a stable door and the latch was highlighted to my eyes. So I walked over and lifted the latch so gently and opened the door. There was no creak or noise, but then the door was wide open and I smiled at the fiery horse within it. As it reared up, it let out a loud roar like noise and bolted out of the stable. God was showing me that I, like many others, had stabled His spirit and prohibited His hand to move. It was never meant to be that way.

I had let the stallion from the stable, His spirit was free to run in my life. But what was I ready to do? What did I have faith to believe for?

Pastor saw something in me, that only my mother had previously seen. A leader. As I grew up, 1 of 6 children, I was the only one she would say "Be a leader, not a follower". My pastor approached me and invited me to be a part of his mentor class. I was beyond excited! I respected my pastor so much and I was thankful for a midweek feeding. Something to spur me on as I chased after God. It was almost like having a cheering section screaming "YOU CAN DO THIS!" I was about to become a Timothy and my Pastor was my Paul.

I looked forward to Wednesday mornings with excitement. I had taken on a second job on Wednesdays, but I quickly left that. I could not put anything before God and what He wanted to do in my life. The best way to describe what was happening, was that the breath of God was blowing on the embers of my heart, I was about to go up in Godly flames.

I would describe what happens next as a Spiritual Spontaneous Combustion. I was hungry for God, more than I had been before. But the usual stuff was not sufficing. I was praying, worshipping and attending church and classes, but I still wanted more. So I began to fast, I had never fasted before and the only thing I knew of fasting was what I had learned as a child. We would not eat anything the first Sunday of every month, as that was our "Fast Sunday". I didn't know you were supposed to pray and seek God while fasting, but thankfully that was what I did. I was learning to depend on food alone.

But He answered and said, "It is written, 'Man shall not live by bread alone, but by every word that proceeds from the mouth of God.'" - Matthew 4:4

I can recall that there were 2 life altering services I attended. I can't recall in which order they happened, so I will do my best to explain them. At one service, it was a Saturday night, and the speaker had just finished. My Pastor had done an altar call, but not like any I had seen before. He had called all those that want a double portion of God, to come forward and they would pray for us. Then we would do what they called a "Fire Tunnel" and those who were prayed for to have a double portion would pray for everyone else going through the tunnel.

I remember when the call came to come for a double portion, my feet moved before my brain could talk me out of it. I had walked up front and fell to my knees. I wanted the double portion. I was hungry for God and wanted more. So, they prayed over me and I remember feeling the fire land on me so strong.

The other service, I was watching from home. The speaker was talking about being baptized in the Holy Spirit and speaking in tongues. It was available, I wanted it. I wanted all that God had for me. So I listened closely and she asked us to repeat words, as I repeated the words I felt nothing different. Then I stopped and just said a syllable, just one. It wasn't even a full word, but I felt the spirit fall on me and I crashed to my knees in my dining room. I was speaking in a language I could not comprehend and I was crying so hard I could not see. I kneeled there, on the floor, for close to 2 hours. I could not stop myself from talking in tongues and I could not speak a normal language.

Wondrous Love

These were the 2 pivotal moments that took place in my life. I did not need to be in a church for them to happen, I only needed guidance and a hunger.

A part of me wants to share more of my story with you, but I think this is the point where the shift needs to take place. I could continue, and give you this amazing story to read, or I could share words with you that could lift you above you circumstance. A testimony means nothing if it does not give you hope or strengthen your walk. I pray at this point, that what i have shared with you enlightens you to a greater perspective of what God has for you. We all have a purpose, greater than we could even imagine. The hardest part is finding that purpose, it's harder the more stuff we fill our lives with it. It was in the moment that I lost my identity that God could show me who I really was.

You see my identity was my son. I was Josh's mom! Everyone I talked to, his school/daycare, friends, everyone called me Josh's mom. The enemy came in and stole my identity, but that gave God the chance to show me that my identity was not in my son, but in Christ Jesus.

As I began to seek Him, before I knew I would need Him, God was guiding me to my identity. We were all created for a certain time. Like a flower would not bloom in the winter, we will not bloom until our time has come. My time was at hand, I believe the enemy knew that. I believe that enemy was trying to destroy who I could be, because of what God created me for and the anointing on my life. I also believe if the enemy had known what I would truly become, he would not have touched my family.

The thief does not come except to steal, and to kill, and to destroy. I have come that they may have life, and that they may have it more abundantly. - John 10:10

Let's talk about identity, for a moment. Because so many of us, have an identity crisis and are struggling with who we really are. If our parents came to us and said, "you have an inheritance, when I die you get all of this" and pointed at a safe full of money. Then they handed you their will and it showed that they are leaving everything to you, would you believe them? Would you take it as truth? Of course, you would!

Then, let's look at God. He said you have an inheritance! When Jesus dies, you will have all of this, and God points to the earth. You will have authority and power over it all. Then He hands you the bible and shows you that it's yours. Would you believe Him?

Cynthia Complese

Sadly, most people don't. Too many of us are not accepting of what God has left as our inheritance and what we are truly worth. I am not writing this, as a new thing. The scriptures say it well enough.

Behold, I give you the authority to trample on serpents and scorpions, and over all the power of the enemy, and nothing shall by any means hurt you. - Luke 10:19

Blessed be the God and Father of our Lord Jesus Christ, who according to His abundant mercy has begotten us again to a living hope through the resurrection of Jesus Christ from the dead, to an inheritance incorruptible and undefiled and that does not fade away, reserved in heaven for you, who are kept by the power of God through faith for salvation ready to be revealed in the last time.
- 1 Peter 1:3-5

With the promises given to us by our Lord and Savior we know we do not need to suffer the things of this earth. We do not need to suffer the pain, sickness and disease that runs wild on earth. I know what you're thinking, "But your son died, how can you believe that?" I tell you that if I knew then what I know now, I have faith in God and Jesus to know that my son would not have died. But because I did not know my identity and all that God has for me, I let my son go. I know my biggest mistake was relinquishing my authority on this earth. Jesus died for me, for all of us, but if I don't actively use my authority then I am giving it back to the thief. The one whom Jesus went and took the keys back from.

I am He who lives, and was dead, and behold, I am alive forevermore. Amen. And I have the keys of Hades and of Death.
- Revelation 1:18

In all honesty, the biggest thing I could tell you, is practice. Do not be afraid to pray, do not be afraid to declare and do not be afraid to tell the enemy to get off you. There were too many times in my life that I just skated by, letting the enemy poke and prod at me. When, if I was in practice of prayer, I would have told the enemy to get off me and that he has no right to me.

Some of you may be concerned at this point. "How dare you talk in such a way!" I tell you that Jesus gave us all authority, but it means nothing if we are not using it. More so it means nothing if we are not using it to glorify our Father and His Kingdom.

Wondrous Love

There is a supernatural boldness that comes when you are "in shape" for prayer. By in shape, I mean in practice. Something you do regularly and are not afraid to do so. I don't mean long drawn out prayers, they don't need to be that. The best prayer, I believe, you can prayer is "Father thank you" or "God, I love you". Simple prayers like that mean so much more than a long drawn out wish list. That build your faith, because in those 3 words, you are not telling God you need anything, but telling Him how you are trusting He will supply all your needs.

And my God shall supply all your need according to His riches in glory by Christ Jesus. - Philippians 4:19

Please do not think that walking this out is hard, because it's not. It's hard to figure it out on your own. I was not brought up trusting on God for everything. I was not taught how to pray in a time of need or how to be thankful for what God was doing. Please do not get me wrong, my parents taught me what they knew, but I tell you there is so much more available than any of us can grab hold of.

I had to learn to trust God, and still do. It's a slow surrender. Years ago, before Josh had passed, I had surgeries that stopped me from getting pregnant. Then Josh graduated before me, and is in Heaven. Now we are believing for a miracle, for a child from God. I didn't know how to trust God when all this started. So I would wake up every morning and get in the shower and say "God, I will trust" over and over and over, until I was crying and kneeling in the shower. Then I would compose myself, get up and get ready for work. I walked away from FedEx into another job. It was better pay and I was excited to be home with my husband more. Little did I know that I would stop attending Sunday services and start struggling with my identity. The fire in me did not fade, but I became lazy in prayer and lazy in what I was doing. My discipline was gone and I had slowly faded out of practice.

I remember waking one morning, several years later, and I heard God tell me "It's time to go home". I had been going to other churches nearby, go in and leave, and watching from home when I could. I was getting back in the swing of things when God told me to go home. I knew what that meant, I needed to get back to my home church.

I had to trust God, even when I didn't know how to trust Him. We would hit obstacles, bumps, and roadblocks. Even more, I would cry out to God "I will trust you!" Some would say that by declaring like that you are showing that you don't trust

Cynthia Complese

God, honestly, I don't care if people know if I don't trust God in an area or two. Maybe that will cause them to intercede for me so that I can learn to trust Him.

The greatest injustice we are doing, as the church, is not being honest with ourselves or to those around us about us. I use the trust example, but it can be anything. If there is some area of your life that you are struggling with, intentionally pray over it. Maybe, it's a person, a job, finances, transportation or just spiritual, then pray "God, I will trust you in this area". I surrender my husband to God every day. I cannot save him nor can I be his umbilical link to God. I can pray for him, but only God can save him. So, every morning, I tell God "I give you my husband. I trust you to take care of him and watch over him."

I am not sharing my prayers to tell you how to pray, but to give an example. I know this walk can have its moments of struggle, but know that the struggle will pass and the triumph will come. Some would tell you it's easy, I'll be honest, for me it's not. It is struggle, but I believe that if you are coming against that much opposition, then God must have something great in store for you. You wouldn't take a $1 bill and lock it in a safe, you would spend it. There wouldn't be that big of a concern if someone stole it, it's only a dollar. But if it was $1 million then you would put it in a bank, where it was safe. You would invest it and try to make it greater. In God's eyes, you are worth more than $1 million, you are priceless. Which means the thief is coming to try to take you. To destroy you and make you worthless. But God said you are worth more than that, more than the birds of the air and the flowers of the earth. You are worth more!

"Are not five sparrows sold for two copper coins? And not one of them is forgotten before God. But the very hairs of your head are all numbered. Do not fear therefore; you are of more value than many sparrows. - Luke 12:6-7

One thing I have seen, over the past few years, is that the one area that is under the most attack is the area you are called to excel. For example, if you are under attack of the mind, then there is a good chance you are called to be a prophet. If it's addiction, I believe you are called to be an evangelist. This is not a blanket, cookie cutter, layout. It's what I have noticed over the past few years. There are exceptions and not everyone fits, which I believe it's how it should be.

Wondrous Love

6
Living Love Loud

Love suffers long and is kind; love does not envy; love does not parade itself, is not puffed up; does not behave rudely, does not seek its own, is not provoked, thinks no evil; does not rejoice in iniquity, but rejoices in the truth; bears all things, believes all things, hopes all things, endures all things. **- 1 Corinthians 13:4-7**

True love only comes from God and knowing God. By spending time with God, we learn to live a life of love, His love through us and touching others. To be able to live and walk in love, means to love everyone no matter what. To always see the best in them, regardless of what history or people say about them. To be able to look past the labels and prior deeds and see their creative value. Love will call you into action.

"A Religious Spirit will walk past the one in the wheelchair and speak instead to the harlot to give the word "take up thy bed and walk" but Relationship with God will HEAL THEM BOTH ! God has called you as Reconciler not Condemner!" - Prophetess Lisa Hicks

When we begin to truly love our neighbor as ourselves, we will move with intent and purpose to all who need us. Jesus was moved with compassion, and so He healed. If you do not love, you will not have compassion. Love and compassion come hand in hand. You can empathize and feel sorry for someone or their situation, but if you don't love them you won't have compassion. I am not saying you won't see people healed, but know the motive of your heart. If you are healing for works, works without love is dead.

Though I speak with the tongues of men and of angels, but have not love, I have become sounding brass or a clanging cymbal. And though I have the gift of prophecy, and understand all mysteries and all knowledge, and though I have all faith, so that I could remove mountains, but have not love, I am nothing. And though I bestow all my goods to feed the poor, and though I give my body to be burned, but have not love, it profits me nothing. - 1 Corinthians 1:1-3

Paul speaks about love in Corinthians, he lays that as a foundation. That we would fully understand that we must walk in love. Words, without love, are just noise. Actions without love, are meaningless and without value. We must first love the one we approach and then give our word or pray. Sometimes the hardest person to love is the one under your roof. The one who sees you raw, and real. The one you can't fake who you are with and you can't hide your actions from. The one that sees the truth, not just hears it. I speak from experience, the greatest thing you can do is learn to walk in love at home. If your focus is walking in love at home, those outside the home will see it. Your actions will speak louder than anything you can ever say to someone who is not saved.

Love, is an action word. In that I mean, it's a word that calls us to act. Love would not let you sit on the sidelines and watch, love would call you into motion. Love would call you into prayer, love would call you to lay hands on the sick. Love would call you to help. True love comes from relationship and in that it comes naturally. I do not say that I walk in perfect love at all times, as God is still doing a work in. But He promises to take from glory to glory into the image of Christ. So then if we walk in relationship with Him, we will learn to love people naturally. You will not need to fake love, but you will just love. Outer appearances will seem like nothing, as you begin to see the Father's view of everyone.

When I was first saved, I remember watching people cross the street and feeling how much He loved them. I would stand in line at the store and feel the Father's love for the person in front of me, for the cashier and the child running up and down aisles. I didn't ask for it, God showed me His love so that I could better understand how much He loved me. For me to be able to love others, I had to understand how much I was loved. Not how much others said I was loved, but I had to feel the love from my Father to know it. People could tell me until they were blue in the face how much I was loved, but until I encountered it, it didn't matter. They were just words.

It was in my living room, as I prayed one morning, that I encountered His love for the first time. I felt the overwhelming love come upon me like a warm blanket. I crumbled at the feeling and wept, because I did not feel worthy of such love. It was the Holy

Wondrous Love

Spirit that spoke to me of how much I was worthy. Not because of anything I had done, but because of everything Jesus did. It made me worthy. Because of the cross the father could not see me as anything other than the finished work.

I had been taught once, that there were tents that were used in ancient times. With these tents, there was an opening that hung in two sections. The spacing at the top allowed them to look out and the center allowed them to pass through. Leaving a perfectly cross shaped opening, that you could look through. This was a visual for me to understand that God can only see us through the cross. The completed work, that is so beautiful and precious.

For God so loved the world that He gave His only begotten Son, that whoever believes in Him should not perish but have everlasting life - John 3:16

Love caused God to act, that He could not leave us on this earth in sin and torment, because He loved us. How then, if we love the Father, could we not act?

I am reminded of my time as a dog trainer. I was at work, and I noticed one of my colleagues was having a difficult time. The girls I was speaking with were chuckling about her issues and anxiety and were waiting for her to have a meltdown. I looked at them stunned and walked away. Moments later I found her in a room, crying. In that moment, love caused me to act. I told her she was going to be ok, and that she needed to grab her coat, because we were going outside and I was going to pray for her. I didn't give her the choice, I didn't ask her if she wanted prayer. I told her I was going to pray for her. It was time for her to not suffer any longer.

We stepped outside, just the two of us and I prayed over her. As I was praying another co-worker joined us. When I was done, I asked how she was feeling. I remember seeing peace in her eyes and she looked better. The tears were stopping and she wasn't shaking anymore. I smiled, we talked briefly and I went back inside. I remember as I was going back in that the enemy tried to convince that they would talk about me behind my back now. Call me a religious fanatic or crazy: I recall saying aloud, "So what?"

I had to declare that I didn't care. Because the enemy was trying to put confusion in my mind so that I wouldn't pray the next she needed it. A few weeks later she sends me a message. "Cynthia please pray for me. I am tired of not being able to function and do normal things." Immediately I prayed and I gave her scriptures to declare over her life. Scriptures that would edify and bring strength. I believe desperation called her to reach out and love responded back.

Love will not judge where you have been. I didn't ask her what she went through, why she felt that way. I stood by until she was calm enough to talk, and then we prayed. Love will cause you to move radically, boldly, and intentionally. When you speak, your words are covered in covenant, when you speak from love. Imagine if you will, your words are pills. They need to be taken in and digested. If we are speaking death over a situation or people, then they are digesting things that will kill them. If we are speaking life, then they will bloom, although the pill may be hard to swallow. However, when you speak life from a place of love, it is spiritually candy coated and easier for them to swallow and digest.

Death and life are in the power of the tongue,
And those who love it will eat its fruit. - Proverbs 18:21

The carnal instinct is to speak death. Our first reaction is to speak death over a situation, but love will lead you to speak life.

Brood of vipers! How can you, being evil, speak good things? For out of the abundance of the heart the mouth speaks - Matthew 12:34

I was once told, *"That which you pursue, you prioritize"*. It was the wisest words ever spoken to me. Because that meant I needed to check my heart. What was I truly seeking. What was the priority in my life. What was I making an idol of that should not be. What did I love, and did I love it more then I loved God? It was a true heart check. Was I speaking life out of habit and not out of love?

There comes a time when things cannot stay as they were. I recall that feeling multiple times in my life. The night before Josh got sick, a few weeks after Josh left for Heaven, in 2011 when I was done with being tormented with bipolar, and those were just the beginning. Life shifts, and the decision to ride the wave or be taken under by it is up to us. When things have to change that is when we fight from our knees. The hardest thing for us to do, is surrender. We want to take control and try to fix everything, and if we can't fix it we want to get rid of it. Love and relationship will encourage you to hold on and pray it through. Relationship with the Father will lead you into pray and trust. One thing I said in passing to a friend was *"Love teaches trust"*. I didn't think that

Wondrous Love

phrase through, it just came out. Afterwards I spent the better part of a week meditating on that phrase.

If someone says, "I love God," and hates his brother, he is a liar; for he who does not love his brother whom he has seen, how can he love God whom he has not seen? - 1 John 4:20

My parents love me, and I trust them. Our children trust us, because they love us. There is a mutual relationship with trust and love, and we need to understand that to trust God, we need to love Him. Like a daughter or son would love and trust their parent, we too should trust God. I know it's not easy for many, but it is an amazing transition once you have learned how. There is no Cookie Cutter Christianity, I can't give you steps 1 - 5 on how to love God or how to trust God. It just doesn't work like that, although somedays I wish it did. I believe, though, that in spending time with the Father you revert back to your youth. In that I mean He brings out the childlike faith that is called for us to walk this out in earnest.

Therefore whoever humbles himself as this little child is the greatest in the kingdom of heaven. - Matthew 18:4

In Psalm 103, David spoke of God's goodness. How he restores us, he spoke highly of the benefits of knowing God. How He heals our diseases and redeems our life from destruction. That we are crowned with lovingkindness and His tender mercies. But then he goes on to say that he restores our youth.

"Who satisfies your mouth with good things,
So that your youth is renewed like the eagle's." - Psalm 103:5

I believe that a restored youth is not just in the physical, but in the emotional sense. Many of the kids I grew up with, had no youth. They spent most of their time working and helping to pay bills from the time they were 16. Other people I know squandered it, they did not enjoy their youth but began to chase after things that took them far from God. I was one of those people. When February 21st came, in 2011, I had gone so far from my walk with God, that I didn't even know if He was real anymore. Since my cry out for Him, God has proven repeatedly how real He is. How faithful He is and how much I can truly trust Him to take care of my every need.

I don't say this from a place of having everything perfect or "all my ducks in a row". I feel my life is far from that, I can be

Cynthia Complese

thankful all my ducks are in the same lake. I am still in a position where I know very little about God, because He is so vast and unending, so that which I know of Him is small in comparison to how great and mighty He is. But what I do know, I have learned from experience. I have come to realize that it's not in how much I know about Him, but in how much I communicate with Him. How often I set time aside to be with Him and close out the world. I find that in spending time with Him I am drawn to His word (the Bible) and I am drawn to worship Him.

When we were children, we barely knew our parents, but we knew that we trusted them. We trusted them to hold us, care for us, and kiss away our boo-boo's and tears. We trusted that if we came running to our earthly parent they would embrace us. It's the same with God. He loves us so much, that He wants to make our injuries go away, and our tears go away. He doesn't want to see us hurting, but just like in the story of the prodigal son, the Father could not stop the son from going and making his own choices. The father welcomed him home when he chose to return. Even know I feel like the Lord dances over us with joy. When we make a break through, or begin to walk in what He has called to do, I can imagine Him dancing about His throne room hooting and hollering, exclaiming "SHE GOT IT!" or "HE GOT IT!" He wants to see us be all that He created and called us to be.

My hearts cry is to be able to be the daughter of God that gives Him a twinkle in His eye when He thinks of me. I believe that God takes time to think about us. He sits on His throne and remembers conversations we have with Him and looks back on things we had done together. I want to make happy memories with my Father. I want to fill up on moments of love with my Father and moments of learning to walk and learning to trust. It's ok to "toddle" around and stumble and learn to get this. It's ok to be wrong and it's ok to make a mistake. Trust that He has you, so close and tenderly in His arms. Trust that He will guide you, and yet be open to being corrected. Those whom He loves He corrects.

> My son, do not despise the chastening of the LORD,
> Nor detest His correction;
> For whom the LORD loves He corrects,
> Just as a father the son *in whom* he delights.
> – Proverbs 3:11-12

Just as my earthly father corrected me when I did wrong and did everything he could to direct me in this thing called life, so

Wondrous Love

does my Heavenly Father wish to help. Sometimes we are so filled with Pride we can't accept that we might need help. Just like when we were 5 or 6 years old and stuck in being able to do things on our own, we scream about being able to do it. "NO, I don't need your help, I can do it myself!" We as adults now scream that and the Heavenly Father. So often God wants to help us with the simplest things, and we scream back at Him we don't need His help. It's chores, doing our hair, folding our clothes or grooming a pet. It's simple, so we justify that we shouldn't need His help. But He wants us to recognize that everything is easier done if we learn to depend on Him.

We are brought up in this world to learn to not depend on anyone, I tell you that having a co-dependency on God is a GOOD THING! I have a co-dependency issue, I am always depending on God to make things easier for me. Jobs I need to get done, wisdom I need in my job and knowledge in communications. I am always relying on God for my day to day as well as the big things. If I can learn to trust Him in the little things, I can trust Him in the BIG moments and the big things.

When I first needed God, I remember I did not listen. I remember that when I heard God's voice, as small soft breeze, I ignored it and brushed it off. The day I found Josh unbreathing, I recall that God tried to get my attention to go back and look in on him. I recall the communication God and I had on it, where He showed me if I had listened the first time, I would have found Josh breathing but unresponsive. I shared this thought with some dear friends and they told me to not think like that. I recall the conversation and they made it seem like it was a horrible thought and I can't even entertain it. This was one of those moments when I knew that it was God that told me, it wasn't me. So, I had to entertain it, I just stopped sharing it.

It wasn't until later that I realized why I had been given this insight. I had to depend on God and His word because I needed to know that every word He shares is life or death. It's not an "if I choose to share" word, someone's life may depend on the word I share. Because of our open communication, and the dependency I have come to have on God, I have become comfortable in sharing what He shares with me. I have learned to steward His word and guard my heart against the world. I want to encourage you to trust that if He shares something with you, it's important. You must trust in Him for this. Again, I know it's easy to read this and feels difficult to do it. But I promise, if you ask Him to help, He is faithful. If you ask Him to teach you to trust Him, He is faithful to teach. He promised to send the teacher, that we may learn. We just need to show up for class.

Cynthia Complese

But the Helper, the Holy Spirit, whom the Father will send in My name, He will *teach* you all things, and bring to your remembrance all things that I said to you. – John 14:26

Wondrous Love

7
Creative Value

"No one can give to anyone else anymore then what they have experienced themselves" - **Kathryn Kuhlman**

My experience with the Father and the Holy Ghost have come from time talking with them. Praying and reading my scriptures. I could say I was seeking Him, but not everyone fully understands what that means. For some that may be singing and praising, others it may be scriptures or maybe even prayer. For me, it's talking with Him, calling out His name and waiting for a response. Not moving until He moves or tells me to move. Remember, relationship will lead to love, which will lead to trust will call you into action.

We hear so much on who we were created to be, but no one truly knows except that person and God. I can't tell you what God made you for, except for what the bible says. To know what God purposed and planned for you in this very moment, is dependent on you seeking Him. I only found my purpose after I was "recreated". I always imagine myself as a lump of clay. I was once form into a vase, functional and did the job it was needed. But it wasn't decorative and it didn't seem like it was in the right spot, but it filled the need. Then after I lost my identity and was broken and recreated, I found that I was a beautiful new vase, created and wonderfully made by the potter's hands. I came to know who I truly was in my time alone with God. While my time alone with Him did not look like that which other people may have, it was my time.

I would be covered in paint and mixtures, oil paint imbedded under my nails and once in a while my husband would ask me how I managed to get paint in an odd place, the back of my neck, my ear, top of my head. I would just chuckle and recall my time with God that day. When I was, young I had minimal artistic skills. My stick figures looked nice and I could draw some cool

Cynthia Complese

things after tracing my hand or using a ruler. But my freehand was not the best. I watched God evolve that into what I have today. What started off small as something to do and to keep my hands busy. Turned into me realizing what I was created for.

I found that I have a love for teaching people. This was whole reason I did so well as a dog trainer. I loved teaching people and I loved seeing what everything finally clicked for them. Didn't matter if they were adults or kids, I wanted to see them succeed. I knew I wanted to teach art, more importantly I wanted to teach prophetic art. I wanted to encourage those around me to stop and listen for God. So, I did that, a few small classes here and there.

I watched as my young students excelled in their childlike faith and I watched as my adult students blossomed before my eyes. The best part, is they were learning more about how God created them and who they were made to be. One of my dear friends took one of my classes, her wardrobe always leaned to the black and white and some earthy tones, but I watched as she painted in pinks and purples. Creating this beautiful masterpiece and learning more about how much of a princess she was.

> I will praise You, for I am fearfully and wonderfully made;
> Marvelous are Your works,
> And that my soul knows very well. - Psalm 139:14

So many scriptures lend to how amazing we are because of how God made us. God created the heavens and the earth, then He made man in His image. I would say in that alone we should know that we are created to create. Not just create life, which is a beautiful miracle of its own, but to create beauty. We create friendships out of nothing, meals out of random ingredients and music out of a rhythm. We were called to create, but the hardest part is what are called to create. Some are called to create a ministry, some are called to create art, maybe you are called to create clothes from bolts of fabric, or to create trust in a person who doesn't know how to. Every day we have the chance to create, you need to decide if you are willing.

I always said God never called the perfect, He called the willing. Those that are willing to walk away from what they knew to walk in what they can't see. To be led by the Holy Spirit from *"glory to glory into the image of Christ"* (2 Corinthians 3:18).

I would like you to take a moment. Just stop and close your eyes. Clear your mind of your to do list and take a deep breath in. Then ask the Holy Spirit to show you the Father's will for you.

Wondrous Love

Did you get anything? Did you get a feeling or an urge? Did you see something? Were you shown a passion that you have kept hidden deep or something that is a hobby that you don't always have time for? Did a memory come to mind and you saw yourself doing something you used to love as a child?

Take a moment and write it down.

_____

_____

_____

_____

_____

I believe that what you saw or felt was your reason for creation. Maybe you saw yourself in worship at church, dancing or singing. This is how it all starts. Learning why we were created and then intentionally putting time into building it. I promise, not all the amazing artists out there were painting masterpieces in a day. It took a leap of faith and a trust that it would get better. No one ever told me that I would create a lot of mistakes in the beginning, but I did.

While I was learning early on, I would stumble and mess up, my art would not come out the way my mind saw it and I would feel down about it. God had to correct me in the middle of a service one Saturday evening, because I was not happy with how this painting had turned out. I heard Him say "*Child, you are just learning to walk. Do not let the bruised knee deter you from walking. You are so close to getting it.*" As the speaker continued to talk I began to cry and ended up stepping out of the service for a moment. I had not thought of how I was still a toddler in this. I was learning how to do what God created me to do, but I had not mastered what He was showing me.

I don't want to tell you to not expect to get it right straight out of the gate, because I pray that God sends you down a path that is already been cleared. For me, I know I am pioneering a way for my family. No one passed me a torch to show me what to do, but I pray that there is someone who already prayed your way through the early steps. Don't get me wrong, I loved every

Cynthia Complese

moment of learning to walk and even the moments I still had to crawl to get where I needed to go. It made the times that I run so much more beautiful to me. The moments when I finish a painting and I stand back, in awe of what He is doing and how amazingly He guides my hand.

God promises to make all things new (*Revelations 21:5*), that is the major point to this chapter. I know many of you that will be reading this will have your walk. The crud and muck you have walked through and the life experiences that have changed you. I don't want you to read this and think that I am telling you to go paint (although I am not opposed to it). I am saying that you should find what you were created for and build on it.

When my son died, I was shattered and broken. That which was my identity was gone and God had the chance to rebuild me, but so did the world. We get to choose who will be laying the building blocks of our faith and our life. I chose to have God lay them out. I could just as easily sat back and let my experiences create me, and define who God was. I could easily hate God or been mad at God and there are those that would have stood beside me and said my emotions were just. But how could I blame God for something that He didn't do?

In making the choice to walk in what we are created for, we are asking God to mold us and shape us. We are telling the things of this world to leave us be and crying out for God to put His hands on the lump of clay that is our lives and mold us. God created each one of you for this time. For this moment, this year, this decade. You were created with a purpose to fulfill a need that only you can do. But you need to ask God to reveal what that is. Some can help you and some may even prophesy over you what they hear God saying. But what someone speaks over you should be the confirming word of what God is already speaking to you. It should confirm the creativity that God has placed in you so that you can be the light in the darkness among those you are supposed to encounter.

I have had many words spoken over me in my life. Some were new words that sent me into prayer to fully understand. Others were confirming the heart cries that only God would hear from me. If someone gives you a word and it's not confirming a word in your heart, then you need to pray about it. God is an amazing Father and friend, He will reveal the truth to you and guide you.

Surely the Lord God does nothing,
Unless He reveals His secret to His servants the prophets.
- Amos 3:7

Wondrous Love

No longer do I call you servants, for a servant does not know what his master is doing; but I have called you friends, for all things that I heard from My Father I have made known to you - John 15:15

Here comes that word again, trust! We should trust that God will reveal to us the secrets of our creation. Only God can call us into a creative position, that is a position that was created for one person specifically. There are many things that I know I was called to fulfill, but I am called into 1 creative purpose.

Imagine if you will a giant jigsaw puzzle. Now on this puzzle all the shapes are the outlines of people. There is one that is your parents, your best friend, your boss, your pastor and so on. Then there is one of you. When we all come to together and fit into our places we interlock with those around us and create an amazing image. But if one piece is not in place, there is a hole. Now someone else might be able to almost fit that spot, maybe their gifting's are the same or they have a heart for similar needs. But the piece just isn't a perfect fit. Now, the place where that person was supposed to fill is now open. It becomes a rough game of piece swapping and place filling. Until God calls another willing person to fill the spot that was meant for someone else. That means that God alters the hole to fit perfectly for someone else.

If we listen closely for our calling, we will find peace and happiness in filling the need we were created for. Recently, at a church service, one of the worshippers had not made it out. She was home sick, but she was our flagger. She would wave flags like a banner, ushering in the spirit of the Lord. This time, however, she was not there. On occasion, I had waved flags instead of paint, but only as the spirit lead. In this instance, I could not bring myself to go paint, I stood back and waved flags. It was during this moment that I hurt my back.

God spent the next week talking to me through this injury and began to show me many things. One morning he began speaking to me on how when people do not trust Him to take care of their every need (illness included), others will break their backs trying to fill the important role they were meant to handle. I was not built for flagging; my body was not prepared for the rigor that the spirit was going to have me do. In that, I hurt myself.

Think of it this way. We are not bodies built for wielding swords anymore. They are heavy and awkward and we don't necessarily have the bicep and forearm strength needed for that. But if your life depended on you picking up a sword and wielding it, you would. Your arms may hurt afterwards and your back might be sore but you would do it. Now, if you are one that was called to wield a sword, then your body would not be in pain and you would be strong enough to wield it. You would have worked using that sword daily and strengthened yourself for it.

It's the same idea in the body of Christ. We are all created for something, to serve a purpose on this earth to glorify God. When one person doesn't step into their position or is unable to, then another who has not trained for it must step in. I am sure if we stop and think about, we will see times in our own lives where we had stepped up to help when we felt less than qualified. Maybe you assisted in something that you weren't sure how to do but were willing to learn. These are all times when we filled a spot meant for someone else, but God used us to help.

Sometimes we will be called in as spiritual space fillers. Ones that hold the place while God gets the person ready. These are times when we step into a position but are only in it for a moment, a month or two, maybe a year and we feel we need to leave. This is those placeholder moments. These are the times when God is preparing someone to step into that place. He is using you to ensure that they will have the ability to go when they are called. I believe He also uses those moments to teach us something we will need later in life as well.

There are those times too when we are called to place hold and then we don't want to leave. God sends an obedient student to let us know. Maybe a prophet comes and says it's time to relocate or you just can't get everything settled in right. Sometimes it can even be a boss coming to you and saying they need to let you go. Or an elder in the church saying you might need to take a step back for a while. It can come in many forms, but that is when God is ready to open the door for the person called to that position and we need to listen for when it's time to let go.

I recall a time I stepped down to edify and encourage another into their calling. I backed down from the stage, after speaking with my pastor. I had let him know that I needed to back down from painting for a while and he had asked one of my students to step in. I was super excited for her. Soon after I was called to spend time at another church. I was there for a season and then left. When I returned to my home church (after a few years) I found that no one was painting again. She had stepped down from painting and no one had filled the spot. I realized then why God had told me to come home.

I quickly went back into my painting position and watched as the spirit moved among the congregation. I realized what I had missed most about being where I was called, that it flowed so effortlessly. I didn't have to fight to paint and I didn't have to struggle to make something happen. I just had to trust in Him that sent me.

I know I am saying that word a lot, *trust*. It's a critical part in knowing God. I do want to talk to you about hope, though. Hope drives us, it leads us into places we thought impossible and strengthens us against the things of this world. Hope is what our faith attaches to. It's what guards our faith so that we see amazing things happen.

By faith Sarah herself also received strength to conceive seed, and she bore a child when she was past the age, because she judged Him faithful who had promised. - Hebrews 11:11

Sarah's faith was attached to hope. Hope that what she had heard so many times from the Lord, would happen. Hope that she would have a child. Because her hope was in the Lord, she knew He would stay true to His word and His promise.

I'm going to give you a little word jargon. Something we should know about the word *hope*. In Hebrews 10:23 the word *hope*, is **elpis**.

Let us hold fast the confession of our hope without wavering, for He who promised is faithful. - Hebrews 10:23

Elpis: Origin- Greek; from a primary elpo (to anticipate, usually with pleasure) Meaning – joyful and confident expectation English Translation – **Hope**

Now faith is the substance of things hoped for, the evidence of things not seen. - Hebrews 11:1

That word hope there is, elpizomenōn, that is "to expect". Now if Faith is the substance of things *expected*, and we are called to have a confident expectation without wavering, then maybe we got hope all wrong.

"And now, Lord, what do I wait for? My hope is in You. - Psalm 39:7

If our hope is in God, then we are looking to God with eager expectations, that do not waver with the day to day. But that are steadfast and trusting in Him that He is faithful in all He will do. I know it's easy to read all of this, but I pray that God speaks to your heart more than your mind as you read this. I would not be

Cynthia Complese

where I am now if not for hope. I was once told that hope means *"Rejoice now for the good is already on its way"*. I was told this just a month or two after my son's passing. I was ready for good. I was ready to see joy return, happiness return. I was ready to see my sorrow turn to dancing. I was ready to be made new and walk this out with strength. When I stopped asking and started rejoicing over words I had been given, I found that I learned to trust God.

I began to see the truth, that it was never about me. My life was never about me, what I went through was never about me and everything I do, it's not about me. It's about God. About bringing glory and honor to His name and representing my family well. It's about not being the "stereotypical" Christian and judging everyone for their sins, but loving them out of sin. It's about speaking in love and trusting the Holy Spirit to move.

I have this amazing Heavenly Father, who loves me and cherishes me. He calls me His daughter; the best part is that He loves you and cherishes you and calls you His own too.

But now, thus says the Lord, who created you, O Jacob,
And He who formed you, O Israel:
"Fear not, for I have redeemed you;
I have called *you* by your name;
You *are* Mine.- Isaiah 43:1

He calls us by name. I think back to when I first called out to God, before I even knew how much I needed Him. I didn't need Him when I cried out, I wanted Him. In return, He called me by name, spoken in the quietest place, sealed in my heart and no one would know if I didn't tell them. I tell you all these things because I want to see you arrive to your full potential. I want to see you hope and trust in the Lord, to be able to count Him faithful in all that He is doing in your life. Because He can do a good work in you! Do not lose your hope, get your hopes up and rejoice. Remember, the good is *already* on its way!

Wondrous Love

Cynthia Complese

About the Author

Cynthia Complese is a passionate pursuer of God. Her walk has not been an easy one. She has conquered some of life's greatest challenges, and came through victorious. As her pastor, I have watched her navigate the trials, and rather than go through the process, she chose to grow through the process. In her pursuit, she has allowed the challenges to drive her closer to God, instead of becoming frustrated or angry at God. Join with her on her journey as you too can experience the true love of the Father who will faithfully walk with all of those who trust in him, through the valleys and on the mountains of life.

Pastor Don Wolabaugh
January, 2017

Cynthia Complese

References

Word definitions from:
  http://www.biblestudytools.com/
  http://biblehub.com/

Bible quotations from the New King James Bible ®. Copyright © 1982 by Thomas Nelson

Harvest Chapel

http://harvestchapelpa.com

Cynthia Complese

Wondrous Love

Cynthia Complese